750 AC
/7

ALEXANDER THE GREAT
A Bibliography

Nancy J. Burich

ALEXANDER THE GREAT

A Bibliography

The Kent State University Press

For Ray

Contents

Preface

Alexander the Great was more than a general, more than a conqueror. Through his efforts, the conquered peoples of Greece, Persia, and India were drawn together. Everywhere his armies went the races were intermingled and customs changed. No land would ever be the same after Alexander's visit. With the increased interest in his accomplishments that has been developing during the past few decades, a collection and evaluation of both ancient and modern sources should provide useful guidance for those who wish to investigate some aspects of his remarkable career. Despite its obvious value for students of Alexander's career no such bibliographic study has previously been attempted.

This annotated bibliography includes only those materials which make a real contribution to the knowledge about Alexander and his exploits. The following types of materials have been deliberately excluded: legend or the "Medieval Alexander," juvenile literature, fiction, drama, poetry, general encyclopedic coverage (i.e., *Encyclopaedia Britannica*, *Collier's Encyclopedia*, *Compton's Encyclopedia*, etc.), general histories, newspaper articles, and general biographical dictionary coverage. These exclusions are made, not because the material is necessarily unimportant, but because it is so vast.

The bibliography is divided into five categories: Bibliographic Aids and General Materials, Classical Sources, Pre-Nineteenth Century Materials, Modern Sources-Monographs, and Modern Sources-Serials. The items are listed in alphabetical order within each section by author or by title if that is better known (e.g. *Cambridge Ancient History*) or if the work is anonymous. Whenever possible each item has been examined first-hand and its general characteristics noted. If the work was not available in the United States, the entry is preceded by an asterisk(*).

It was felt that an evaluation of serial publications would be unnecessary, and therefore only general characteristics have been noted. An evaluation of classical sources is given in the introduction; a further evaluation is not made in the body of the bibliography. Those reference materials which have been included were evaluated by Constance M. Winchell in her *Guide to Reference Books*.[1] Evaluation of each monographic item is based on published reviews written by reputable historians. Where conflicting reviews were located, significant disagreements are noted, but when no reviews were found, the author's qualifications are given instead. The final evaluation of each item was examined and appraised by Professor William L. Wannemacher, professor of ancient history at Kent State University.

Whereas the "Medieval Alexander" was excluded from this work, other pre-nineteenth century materials have been listed but not evaluated. There are several reasons for the omission of annotations for these items: many of these older materials were not available for examination and critical appraisals of the works do not exist; moreover, this was the period when the Alexander legend was being expanded, so that it is very difficult to determine which is part of the romance and which is historical.

Every attempt has been made to include all relevant materials. National bibliographies have been checked to include as many editions of a work as possible, but translations into languages other than English have not been included. For materials written in a foreign language, the original language is used in the citation, except for those published in either the cyrillic or Greek alphabets for which a transliteration is given.

No bibliography is ever complete, and this is no exception. There have been many limitations on this work; the primary one has been time. Because of this, many works have been included which were not examined personally. Therefore, no evaluations of these works have been included. Another problem has been the incorrect or incomplete citation taken from another source. When it has been impossible to verify such items, they have been excluded. In general, the bibliography adheres to customary patterns of organization and annotation.

The compilation of a work such as this requires the help and encouragement of many people. Foremost among these have been Professor William L. Wannemacher; Professor Richard E. Chapin,

[1] Constance M. Winchell, *Guide to Reference Books*. 8th. ed. (Chicago: American Library Association, 1967).

Director of Libraries at Michigan State University; Mrs. Florence F. Hickok, Head of the Reference Library at M.S.U.; and Mr. Walter W. Burinski, Inter-library Loan Librarian at M.S.U., and his assistants, Mrs. Pat Johnson and Mrs. Debbie Johnson.

N.J.B.

Introduction

Primary sources provide the foundation for the study of any period in history. When considering ancient sources, the evaluation becomes more than simply a quantitative-qualitative analysis. In many instances works which have been lost for centuries or remain only in broken fragments must be assessed in light of what other authors have said about them. In addition, the ancient secondary sources vary in quality and must be evaluated for accuracy. This is not always easy since it was common for an author in antiquity to quote something out of context —often necessary when only fragments remain—or to misquote another source. Frequently sources were used without identification or were used inaccurately. However, when even a few small fragments remain, evaluation of some sort is possible. Whenever the full text remains, the evaluations which have been made by others can be assessed and accepted or rejected.

The first group of materials to be evaluated here is that of the so-called "lost historians," authors whose works have completely disappeared or survive in fragments only. One such contemporary record of the life and adventures of Alexander is the *Royal Journal of Alexander the Great* or the *Ephemerides*. This was a candid, detailed, and truthful record of personal, military, and administrative memoranda begun not later than 336 B.C. and may have been inherited from Alexander's father, Philip. It was kept by Eumenes of Cardia and his assistant, Diodotus of Erythrae. It is possible that this was the ultimate basis for the so-called "official tradition" of which Arrian speaks. Although Arrian seems to have had access to the full text of the *Journal*, only fragments remain today. Fortunately, these fragments have been collected by Felix Jacoby.[2] Because this type of document was not meant to heighten or glorify the achievements of Alexander, most

[2] Felix Jacoby, *Die Fragmente der Griechischen Historiker* (Berlin, 1930). III (1955), 429-55.

xiii

historians believe the *Journal* to have been an accurate account of everyday events. However, as often happens when only fragments of a work remain, added pieces have been introduced over the years for various purposes. In fact, it is believed that such forged fragments were in existence by the time of Arrian (c96-180 A.D.). A discussion of the entire question of the *Journal* and the added fragments is found in Lionel Pearson's article, "The Diary and Letters of Alexander."[3]

The next of the "lost historians," in chronological order from the assumed date of birth, is Callisthenes (c372 B.C.-328 B.C.). He is believed to have been the nephew of Aristotle and is also ranked as one of the most famous historians of ancient times. He accompanied Alexander on the invasion of Persia in 334 B.C. and was charged with writing a history of the expedition. His history, *Hellenica*, pictured Alexander as a champion of Panhellenism, partly as propaganda against the Greek opposition at home. Today Callisthenes is considered responsible for the romantic narrative of Alexander's life which later developed. Having accompanied Alexander on the expedition and having had access to official records, one might assume that the purpose of his history was for the dissemination of propaganda and not to provide an accurate historical record of events. Callisthenes further attempted to please Alexander through an identification of Homeric sites, equating his travels with those of the Homeric heroes. The inaccuracies and outright misrepresentations in these identifications are numerous. Just how numerous we will probably never know, since only fragments of the *Hellenica* remain today. These have been collected, translated into German, and interpreted by Jacoby.[4] Callisthenes' re-creation of the travels of Alexander ended in 327 B.C. when he quarrelled with Alexander and fell from grace. An added incentive to having him imprisoned may have been his unwillingness to humble himself before Alexander in the oriental fashion. Callisthenes never returned from the expedition. Whether he was later executed or died from illness is not known, but he has since become an almost legendary figure.

Another contemporary figure, and a more trustworthy historian, who accompanied Alexander to Asia was Hieronymous of Cardia (370 B.C.-c272 B.C.). His history was the most important source for the period from the death of Alexander to the death of Pyrrhus (272 B.C.), but it remains today only in fragments which were collected by Carl

[3] Lionel Ignacius Cusack Pearson, "The Diary and Letters of Alexander," *Historia*, III (1955), 429–55.

[4] Felix Jacoby, *Die Fragmente*.

Müller a century ago.[5] Hieronymous was used as the chief source for
the period by Arrian (c96-180 A.D.) and Diodorus (first century B.C.),
and these in turn were the chief sources used by Plutarch (c46-c120
A.D.). However, it is impossible to determine the extent to which his
history of Alexander was followed by either Diodorus or Plutarch.
His writing style was criticized by Dionysius, and he was censured by
Pausanias for his partiality to Antigonus and Demetrius, under whom he
served as a soldier, and for his injustice to Pyrrhus and Lysimachus,
whom he held responsible for the destruction of his home city,
Cardia. If these criticisms were justified, it would seem as though
Hieronymous was guilty of changing incidents and characters of people
to suit his own ends. Since the full text of his work is no longer available, the extent of his deficiencies cannot be determined, but as long as
the full text remained Hieronymous was the single most important
source for the period.

A third contemporary of Alexander was Ptolemy, son of Lagus
(367 B.C.-283 B.C.), who later became king of Egypt. He was one of
the personal attendants of Alexander and attained the rank of general
while the expedition was in India. He was given the province of Egypt
and Libya by Alexander and became king in 305 B.C. It was he who
relaid the foundations of wealth and prosperity in Egypt, restored order,
and advanced the cause of literature and science through the creation
of the Library and Museum of Alexandria. During his own lifetime, he
was well known for his political wisdom, ambition, and long-sighted
prudence. A few years before his death in 283 B.C., Ptolemy began an
historical narrative of the wars of Alexander in an attempt to correct
the romantic stories about Alexander which had been developing since
before his death. The history of Ptolemy was notable for the absence of
fables, exaggerations, and miraculous elements. His sources included
the official *Journal*, other official documents and his own recollections. His
accounts were trustworthy with rare exceptions. In fact, some believe that
his was the best of the Alexander histories. The few fragments which
remain today may be found in Jacoby's collection of fragments.[6] Arrian
must have had access to the entire text, because Ptolemy was one of his
major sources. Ptolemy's accounts are rarely questioned because, as
Arrian pointed out, Alexander was dead and Ptolemy had nothing to

---

[5] Carl Müller, *Fragmenta Historicum Graecorum* (Paris, 1841-70).
[6] Felix Jacoby, *Die Fragmente.*

gain through lying. However, it is not unlikely that he somewhat exaggerated his own part in the Alexander saga.

Aristobulus also accompanied Alexander on his campaign and, like Ptolemy, wrote a reliable history of Alexander during the later years of his life. He was eighty-five years old when he wrote his careful observations on the campaigns of Alexander. His history, now lost except for a few fragments, was highly praised for its trustworthiness, but he was more accurate on geography and natural history than on military or political matters. His work was not always critical, but he took pains to be consistent in his characterizations. He used first-hand information, having been a companion to Alexander and a technician in the army during the Asiatic conquests. Because only fragments of his history remain,[7] there has been a great deal of question about the order in which he, Ptolemy, and Callisthenes wrote their histories. It is the opinion of many experts, among them Tarn and Pearson, that Aristobulus wrote before both Ptolemy and Callisthenes.[8] Aristobulus was used by Arrian to supplement the work of Ptolemy, by Strabo as the basis for his *Alexander in India*, and by Athanaeus, Plutarch, and Q. Curtius Rufus as one of their many sources. Unlike many of the ancient writers who were trying to advance the romance of Alexander through exaggerations, Aristobulus was cautious when reporting the size and numbers of military forces. His was a trustworthy and accurate picture of Alexander's exploits.

A different type of history was written by Chares of Mytilene. Having been Alexander's chamberlain or officer in charge of audiences, he was able to relate matters concerning the court. His *Stories of Alexander* in ten books contained passages to illustrate the luxurious habits of Alexander and reminiscences to show the changes in the character of Alexander before and after the conquest of Darius' empire. The history contained nothing on military matters except when they were mentioned to illustrate another point. In spite of the fact that his *Stories* was full of court ceremonial and personal gossip, it had the reputation of being trustworthy and interesting. Unfortunately, this document has survived in small fragments only. These are available in Latin translation in the Young collection.[9]

[7] Felix Jacoby, *Die Fragmente.*
[8] For a discussion of this question see William Woodthrope Tarn, *Alexander the Great* (Cambridge: Cambridge University Press, 1948), 31-6, 28, 38, 42-3.
[9] Douglas Young, ed., *Theognis, Ps.-Pythagoris, Ps.-Phocylides, Chares, Anonymi Aulodia Fragmentum Teliambicum* (Lipsiae: B.G. Teubneri, 1961).

Another member of this group and one who was not a contemporary of Alexander is Cleitarchus of Alexandria. This Alexander historian was a secondary writer who never knew Alexander or travelled to Asia. His writing was done during the time of Ptolemy II, after 280 B.C. His sources were many—Aristobulus, Nearchus, Chares, Callisthenes, Aristobulus, and his father Dinon—but his chief sources seem to have been popular belief and imagination. He was notoriously untrustworthy, believed in the marvelous, and improved facts for the sake of dramatic effect. It may be this attention to the "good" story which made him one of the most popular writers for the general reading public of the Ciceronian Age, but the more critical writers of antiquity strongly expressed opposing opinions. Cicero judged his ability greater than his veracity, Longinus called his style frivolous, and Strabo called him an outright liar. In spite of these judgments, his work was used as the main authority for the narratives of Trogus Pompeius and Q. Curtius Rufus, although he was censured by Curtius for certain inaccuracies. It is unfortunate that this interesting twelve-book work on Alexander has survived only in fragments.[10]

The authors discussed above do not constitute a complete list of writers whose works concerning Alexander remain in fragmentary form, but they are the most important ones. An entire section of Jacoby's collection is devoted to all fragments concerning Alexander available to him at the time of publication (1923–30). When the works themselves are still available in complete or nearly complete form, the methods of testing the credibility of the sources they used and the accuracy with which they used these sources are less difficult. However, if the sources used by ancient historians have been lost, the evaluation involves the same problems encountered in the attempt to judge the "lost historians." Nevertheless, as long as the complete work exists, there can be no question of it being quoted incorrectly. Furthermore, evaluations can be made by all who read the work.

The earliest of those historians whose works have not been lost is Nearchus who lived from about 350 B.C. to about 312 B.C. He was both Alexander's friend and confidential adviser and accompanied him on the Indian expedition as the commander of the fleet. In this capacity, Nearchus travelled along the Indus, Tigris, and Euphrates rivers and discovered their mouths. His honest and trustworthy chronicle is not

[10] These fragments are found in Felix Jacoby, *Die Fragmente.*

a history of Alexander, but rather an account of their travels in India. Even though it was not meant to be a testimonial for Alexander, it is the most convincing and sympathetic picture by a contemporary that has survived from ancient times. The account is rich in its description of geographical discoveries, but Nearchus drew on Herodotus and the *Odyssey* for literary touches to improve and to illustrate his story. His account of India was used by both Arrian and Strabo. His honesty and integrity in political matters were illustrated when he, remaining loyal to Alexander even after the latter's death, faithfully governed the provinces entrusted to him. Alexander could not have had a better friend and biographer had he been able to foresee the future and control it.

An eminent historian of the first century B.C. was Diodorus Siculus. He lived under both Caesar and Augustus and travelled for many years in Europe and Asia to collect material for a universal history. It is reported that he spent thirty years in writing his forty-book *Historical Library*, which he completed about 10 B.C. Only fifteen books have been preserved in their entirety. This work is in the form of annual accounts which end in 60 B.C.; its primary value lies in its vastness, detail, and chronology. The chronology is good for the period of Alexander, containing only occasional errors due to the authorities he chose to follow. Another virtue is the fact that it contains materials from authors whose works no longer exist. However, these virtues are balanced by a number of deficiencies. The history is a collection of authorities jumbled together with no critical judgment or evaluation, and any such compilation is only as reliable as its sources. The result is a combination of history, myth, and fiction indiscriminately mixed together. Even when the sources used had some merit, Diodorus frequently misunderstood or mutilated them and contradicted himself. But perhaps his main fault was in the selection of so broad a subject.

Probably the best-known and most often read of the ancient authors is the Greek biographer Plutarch, who was born about 46 A.D. and died around 120 A.D. During his lifetime Plutarch travelled widely throughout Italy, taught in Rome, and studied philosophy under Ammonius at Delphi. His main interests were ethics and philosophy. He admired the philosophy of Plato and was the opponent of Epicureanism. He is best known for his *Parallel Lives*, although he is the author of some sixty additional works. The *Lives* is a series of character studies of distinguished Greeks and Romans who lived from the time of Theseus and Romulus to his own time. In delineating character traits, important historical events often were subordinated to anecdotes which revealed aspects of personality. In addition, the order of time or chronology is often purposely neglected. Nevertheless, the portraits he painted have become the generally accepted images of the great historical figures he described. The *Lives* display an impressive amount of learning and research, but Plutarch included in his sources anecdote-mongers and writers of memoirs, as well as historians. It is said that he quoted from more than two hundred and fifty writers of whom eighty represent works that have since been lost. This would seem to indicate the availability of large numbers of books and manuscripts concerning both the Greeks and Romans. However, in spite of all these materials, he was imperfectly informed on Roman institutions and the men he sought to describe. This was partially due to his imperfect knowledge of Latin. He often used secondary Greek sources which were not always accurate. In addition, Plutarch felt that the Greek way of life was superior to that of the Roman. Nevertheless, he rarely conveyed erroneous notions. Many would say that he was the greatest biographer of antiquity. Certainly very few reputations have been sustained as long as his.

A military picture of Alexander was painted by Arrian (c96-c180 A.D.). He was the first Greek to rate a Roman military command, and Hadrian appointed him governor of Cappadocia from 131 to 137 A.D. and archon from 147 to 148 A.D. A biography of Arrian written by Dio Cassius is now lost. Arrian's most important work, the *Anabasis of Alexander*, is a history of the life of Alexander from his accession to his untimely death. Arrian's sober narrative, which is said to be the most reliable ancient source for information concerning the military career of Alexander, clearly allows his practical knowledge of military affairs to show through. His chief authorities, Aristobulus and Ptolemy, had both traveled with Alexander and had had access to the most reliable information. They were certainly the most reliable sources available to him. Arrian was a real historian, not simply a compiler. He used good judgment, was accurate in geographical and strategical details, and was an excellent historical critic. He had a correct and simple literary style similar to that of Xenophon, his literary model. As a supplement to his seven-book *Anabasis*, he abstracted Nearchus' account of the expedition through India and appended it to his work. Together, these two works form the most complete and reliable account of Alexander's travels.

Q. Curtius Rufus was a Latin biographer of Alexander who lived
during the first century B.C. Although little is known about his life,
anyone with the most elementary knowledge of geography, tactics,
or astronomy could say with some assurance that Curtius knew little
about these subjects. He showed such partiality for the hero of his study
—Alexander—that his work became a series of brilliant and romantic
adventures far removed from reality. His sources included Cleitarchus,
Timagenes, Ptolemy, Aristobulus, and even some anti-Alexander
material. If he had really wanted to glorify Alexander, as he seemed
to want to do, one would think that his historical insight and critical
judgment would have eliminated the last category of materials from his
consideration, but it was included apparently because his main aim was to
be dramatic and not historical.

The final ancient author to be considered here was as unreliable an
historian as the preceding one. Critics can find little merit in his work
except for its literary style. The author is Justin, who lived in the
third century A.D., and his work is the *Historiarum Philippicarum
Libri XLIV.* The work was intended to be an abridgement of the *History
of the World* written by Trogus Pompeius. Justin tried to overlook
the commonly-known in favor of the more obscure. In doing so, he
spread incoherence and inequality throughout the abridgement. However, he seems to have used extensive research and drew heavily from
Greek sources and from Theopompus for the title and general plan of his
work. But this does not compensate for the fact that the work has
little historical merit.

The preceding survey is by no means a comprehensive evaluation of
all the ancient authors who have written about Alexander and his
contributions to history. Such a task would be beyond the scope of a
study such as this, and it would be nearly impossible to discuss all those
who have, at one time or another, mentioned Alexander in their writings. In the same manner, it would be even more difficult to examine
all the modern works which have evaluated Alexander and his period
in history. Probably every textbook dealing with the history of the
ancient world mentions him; but four authors in the present century
have written major works concerning Alexander and the Hellenistic Age.
It is these men who have helped to shape the thinking of other modern
historians and students of ancient history. These men, their works and
ideas, will be considered here as they apply to an evaluation of materials
concerning Alexander's career. Such an appraisal of modern biographies

and histories is less complicated than an evaluation of ancient sources since in most cases we can examine the sources used, the works themselves come to us intact and without intervening translations, and the authors can be questioned when any passage seems obscure or questionable. Whereas few ancient authors have given us interpretations of their works, each of these four modern authors have on numerous occasions explained their works in scholarly journals. The four historians to be considered here are: Charles Alexander Robinson, Jr., Michael Ivanovich Rostovtzeff (Mikhail Ivanovich Rostovsev), Sir William Woodthrope Tarn, and Ulrich Wilcken.

The first of the modern Alexander-historians is Charles Alexander Robinson, Jr., who died in 1966 at the age of sixty-six. Professor Robinson was an archaeologist and professor of the classics at Brown University. He studied at the American School of Classical Studies at Athens and at the American Academy of Rome. To say that he engaged in extensive research and writing concerning Alexander and the Hellenistic Age would be an under-statement. His works have ranged from *Alexander the Great; the Meeting of East and West in World Government and Brotherhood*[11], which is suitable for the general adult reader, to *The Ephemerides of Alexander's Expedition*[12], which is a specialized scholarly study. His *History of Alexander the Great*[13] is a general work dealing with source materials used by both extant and "lost" ancient historians. Through periodical articles, Robinson dealt with various phases of Alexander's character and military career.[14] In addition, he wrote many book reviews and a short study of Tarn's work concerning Alexander.[15] His final publication—*History of Alexander the Great*—appeared in 1962.

Michael Ivanovich Rostovtzeff was an American classicist who was born in Kiev, Russia, in 1870. Following a distinguished career in Europe and a brief period at the University of Wisconsin, he became a professor of Latin, Roman history and ancient history and archaeology at

---

[11] Charles Alexander Robinson, Jr., *Alexander the Great; the Meeting of East and West in World Government and Brotherhood* (N.Y.: Dutton, 1947).

[12] Charles Alexander Robinson, Jr., *The Ephemerides of Alexander's Expedition* (Providence, R.I.: Brown University Press, 1932).

[13] Charles Alexander Robinson, Jr., *History of Alexander the Great* (Providence, R.I.: Brown University Press, 1962).

[14] For specicfic references, see the appended bibliography.

[15] Charles Alexander Robinson, Jr., "Alexander's Plans: Based on W.W. Tarn's Papers," *American Journal of Philology*, XLI (1940), 401–12.

Yale University. After his retirement, he was given the status of professor emeritus and received honorary degrees from Oxford, Harvard, Athens, Cambridge, and Chicago universities. His works are varied and deal with many aspects of the ancient world. His *Social and Economic History of the Hellenistic World*[16] is complementary to a similar work on the Roman Empire.[17] Both are standard studies of ancient social and economic history. Rostovtzeff was also the author of a more general history which utilized fully his great historical talents—his *History of the Ancient World*.[18] Many of his periodical articles are concerned with the economic and social development of the Hellenistic period.[19] Active writing and publication ended in 1941, although he lived until 1955. His books are the authority any specialist or student of ancient history should consult for information concerning the economic and social conditions of the Hellenistic period.

The third of the modern historians is Sir William Woodthrope Tarn (1869-1957). He received his degree from Cambridge University and was awarded an honorary degree from the University of Edinburgh. In addition, he was made a Fellow of the British Academy. Probably his greatest contributions to the study of Alexander and the Hellenistic Age are represented in his chapters of the *Cambridge Ancient History*.[20] Tenny Frank, who considered Tarn one of the outstanding students of Alexander, rated these chapters as among the author's best works.[21] The first volume of Tarn's biography of Alexander,[22] is an enlargement of his chapters in the *Cambridge Ancient History* modified to appeal to the general adult reader. The second volume, a collection of essays on the problems and sources of the Alexander story, is an indispensable tool for the professional scholar. Together these two volumes make a very real contribution to the study of Alexander. Tarn's other works,

---

[16] Mikhail Ivanovich Rostovtzeff, *Social and Economic History of the Hellenistic World* (Oxford: At the Clarendon Press, 1941).

[17] Mikhail Ivanovich Rostovtzeff, *Social and Economic History of the Roman Empire*. 2d. rev. ed. by P.M. Fraser (Oxford: Clarendon Press, 1957).

[18] Mikhail Ivanovich Rostovtzeff, *History of the Ancient World* (Oxford: Clarendon Press, 1928-30).

[19] For a list of articles, see the appended bibliography.

[20] *Cambridge Ancient History* (Cambridge: The University Press, 1927), Vol. VI.

[21] Tenny Frank, *Books* (*New York Herald Tribune*), December 11, 1927, p. 2.

[22] William Woodthrope Tarn, *Alexander the Great* (Cambridge: Cambridge University Press, 1948).

in both book and periodical form, dealing with either Alexander or the Hellenistic Age, examine the civilization in general and its military developments. But each of these later works is an expansion of the work begun in 1927.

The last, but by no means the least, of the modern historians to be considered here is Ulrich Wilcken (1862-1939) who received his Ph.D. at the University of Berlin in the field of ancient history. An historian of broad interests, he did not confine himself to the study of Alexander and the Hellenistic Age, but Robinson rated his *Alexander the Great*[23] as the best biography in the field at the time of its publication.[24] This biography discusses the aims and psychology of Alexander and sketches his influence on history. Wilcken's conclusions are based on his investigation of the original authorities and on a close study of modern discoveries. Like other scholars discussed here, Wilcken wrote extensively in scholarly journals.

These then are four leading historians who are firmly established through their significant contributions to materials concerning Alexander the Great and the Hellenistic Age. But this group is by no means a closed one. Others have entered the field and are enriching our understanding of Alexander and the Hellenistic Age. One of these scholars who is in the process of establishing himself as a leading historian is Ernst Badian. He has already published several books and many journal articles. Like the other modern historians discussed, Badian's interest in ancient history seems to be general and not confined to either Alexander or the Hellenistic Age. His works have been as broad as his *Studies in Greek and Roman History*[25] or as specialized as the article, "Egypt Under the Ptolemies."[26] If the literary pace with which he has begun is continued, he will certainly join the group of eminent historians in the field of ancient history.

[23] Ulrich Wilcken, *Alexander the Great*, tr. by G.C. Richards (N.Y., Dial Press, 1932).

[24] Charles Alexander Robinson, Jr., *Saturday Review of Literature*, October 1, 1932, p. 147.

[25] Ernst Badian, ed., *Studies in Greek and Roman History* (Oxford: Basil Blackwell, 1964).

[26] Ernst Badian, "Egypt Under the Ptolemies," *History Today*, X (July, 1960), 451-9.

I. Bibliographic Aids and General Materials

1 *ABS International Guide to Classical Studies*. Darien, Conn.: American Bibliographic Service, 1961- . A quarterly index to periodicals, which with vol. 6 includes annuals, festschriften, and symposia; listings by author and subject.

2 Altheim, F. *Weltgeschichte Asiens im Griechischen Zeitalter*. 2 vols. Halle: M. Niemeyer, 1947-48. Many notes, illustrations, maps, an index (in vol. 2), and comparisons of the texts of Diodorus, Plutarch, Arrian, and Curtius Rufus. An excellent survey by a well-known scholar.

3 *L'Année Philologique*; *Bibliographie Critique et Analytique de l'Antiquité Gréco-Latin*. Paris: Société d'Édition "Les Belles Lettres," 1928- . An annual survey in classified order covering the period 1927 to date; a continuation of Marouzeau.

4 Arnim, Hans Friedrich August von, ed. *Stoicorum Veterum Fragmenta*. 3 vols. Lipsiae: B.G. Teubner, 1903-05. Reprinted by the same publisher in 1921-23. A fourth volume by M. Adler was published by the same company in 1924. All 4 volumes reprinted by Teubner in 1967. Vol. 4 contains the indexes for the set. Each of the first three volumes contains a table of contents, texts of the fragments, and a commentary. An excellent set by an eminent Hellenic philologist.

5 Babelon, Ernest [Charles François]. *Melanges Numismatiques*. 2 vols. Paris: Chez C. Rollin et Feuardent, 1892-93. Mostly reprints from various serials. Contains a list of publications by the author,

a table of contents listing the journal citations, a family tree, illustrations, and comparative tables.

6 Badian, Ernst, ed. *Ancient Society and Institutions; Studies Presented to Victor Ehrenberg on His 75th. Birthday.* Oxford: Blackwell and Mott, 1966. N.Y.: Barnes and Noble, 1967. A vita and short bibliography of Ehrenberg, many notes, but unfortunately no index. An especially important compilation of articles with an emphasis on Greek history, mostly by eminent British classicists. A volume worthy of the great scholar whom it honors.

7 Beloch, Karl Julius. *Griechische Geschichte.* 3 vols. in 4. Strassburg: K.J. Trübner, 1893-1904. 2d. ed. by the same publisher in 1912-27 as 4 vols. in 8 (v. 3, pt. 1 & 2, Berlin and Leipzig: W. de Gruyter, 1922-23. v. 4, pt. 1 & 2, Berlin and Leipzig: W. de Gruyter, 1925-27). A good bibliography which is international in scope, a detailed index, a chronological table down to 639 A.D., a list of Persian and Hellenistic kings, a genealogical table for the Hellenistic royal families, and 6 maps. A general handbook which gives a thorough criticism of all sources and includes a survey of modern scholarship.

8 Bengtson, Hermann. *Griechische Geschichte von den Anfängen bis in der Römische Kaiserzeit.* Handbuch der Altertumswissenschaft, III. Munich: C.H. Beck, 1950. Includes a mass of bibliographical material in its many notes and brief bibliographies and general summaries which begin each section, chronologies and family trees for monarchs, a chronology for 2300 B.C. to 639 A.D., fold-out colored maps, and an extensive index. A survey of modern scholarship giving a balanced view of achievements in international research. According to H. W. Parke, Bengtson's general tendency is to overstress the importance of Persian influence in Greek history. The volume's chief contribution is in the later development and diffusion of Greek culture.

9 ———. *Die Strategie in der Hellenistischen Zeit. Ein Beitrag zum Antiken Staatsrecht.* Münchener Beiträge zur Papyrusforschung und Antiken Rechtsgeschichte, 26. 3 vols. Munich: Beck, 1937-52. Reprinted by the same publisher in 1964-67. An expanded table of contents in each volume, notes, and an index. A most

valuable work by a scholar who is clearly in full command
of the subject.

10 Berve, Helmut. *Gestaltende Kräfte der Antike: Aufsätze und
Vortrage zur Griechischen und Römischen Geschichte.* Munich:
C. H. Beck, 1949. 2d. much enlarged ed.
by Edmund Buchner
and Peter Robert Franke, by the same publisher in 1966.
No footnotes or bibliography or index. A collection of 8 essays
designed for a relatively unspecialized audience. The second
edition, published in honor of the author's 75th. birthday, has 7
additional essays that are a bit antiquated. The original 8 essays
have been undated. A review by Stewart I. Oost states that,
". . . one particularly deplores the absence of footnotes . . .
especially since scholars may want to question some of the author's
interpretations."

11 ———. *Griechische Geschichte.* 2 vols. Freiburg: Herder, 1931-34.
2d. ed. by the same publisher in 1951-52, and reprinted by them
in 1959-60. Plates, a bibliography in each volume, an index in
vol. 2, but no footnotes. A survey of the manifestations of
civilization in its entirety. Written with enthusiasm and containing
many new ideas and interpretations. According to W. S. Ferguson,
the result of Berve's method is ". . . a schematization rhetorically
effective perhaps but scientifically highly objectionable." In spite of
this judgment, Ferguson called it an intelligent, impressionistic,
and controversial book, the work of a gifted man.

12 Blass, Friedrich. *Die Attische Beredsamkeit.* 3 vols. in 4. Leipzig:
B. G. Teubner, 1868-80. 2d. ed. by the same publisher in 1878-98.
A table of contents, notes, and an index in each volume. A collection of texts divided by person by one of the foremost Greek
scholars in Europe in the nineteenth century; the greatest of
his works.

13 Boeckh, August, ed. *Corpus Inscriptionum Graecarum.* 4 vols. in 8.
Berlin: Ex Officina Academica, 1828-77. The texts of inscriptions
with notes. A great achievement in pure scholarship; a truly
monumental work.

14 Borchardt, Ludwig. *Allerhand Kleinigkeiten.* Berlin: Privatdruck,
1933. Table of contents, illustrations, notes, and the texts
of inscriptions.

15　Brown, Truesdell S., ed. *Ancient Greece.* Sources in Western
　　Civilization, vol. II. [N. Y.]: Free Press of Glencoe, [c1965].
　　An introductory essay, translations of classical fragments, and
　　rudimentary notes. A series intended for those with no classical
　　background to give them a fair idea of ancient historiography.

16　Bunbury, Edward Herbert. *A History of Ancient Geography
　　Among the Greeks and Romans from the Earliest Ages till the
　　Fall of the Roman Empire.* 2 vols. London: J. Murray, 1879.
　　2d. ed. by the same publisher in 1883. N. Y.: Dover Publications,
　　1959. Many footnotes, maps, and an extensive index. The 1959
　　edition is a reprint of the second edition of 1883. With its
　　elaborate detail and numerous digressions, it is on a scale adapted
　　to the needs of advanced scholars. H. F. Tozer termed it ". . . a book
　　equally conspicuous for learning and for judgment, and one
　　which . . . will not readily be superseded."

17　Bury, John Bagnell. *Ancient Greek Historians.* N. Y. and London:
　　Macmillan, 1909. A bibliography, an index, and many notes.
　　An historical survey of Greek historiography down to the first
　　century B.C.; presented as the Lane Lectures at Harvard in 1908.
　　A valuable supplement to his *History of Greece.* His criticism of
　　Herodotus and Thucydides superseded all earlier handbooks.

18　———. *A History of Greece to the Death of Alexander the Great.*
　　2 vols. N. Y. and London: Macmillan, 1902. Rev. ed. London:
　　Macmillan, 1913. N. Y.: Modern Library, [1937]. 3d. ed. rev. by
　　Russell Meiggs. London: Macmillan, 1952. Many maps and
　　diagrams, a chronological table, and references and notes. The work
　　has been criticized for being dull and having a poor arrangement
　　of material, and portraying poor historical sense. It has been
　　thoroughly revised and the changes have been made without
　　altering pagination of the second edition. The notes have been
　　increased and include summaries of evidence. The illustrations are
　　numerous and excellent.

19　*Cambridge Ancient History.* Ed. by J. B. Bury, S. A. Cook, and
　　F. E. Adcock. 12 vols. Cambridge, England: The University Press,
　　1923-39. Many footnotes, chronologies, a bibliography, and
　　5 separate volumes of plates. Chapters written by experts in
　　historical research; authoritative, well-documented.

20 *Cambridge History of India.* Ed. by E. J. Rapson. 6 vols. Cambridge: University Press, 1922-64. An index in each volume, a list of abbreviations, a general bibliography and one following each chapter, plates, maps, notes, and a summary of numismatic evidence. A cooperative effort with each section treated by a scholar equipped to do justice to it. Well edited to coordinate the whole, but it has been criticized as a ". . . mere rehashing and redigesting of old fallacies and prejudices."

21 Cary, Max. *The Geographic Background of Greek and Roman History.* Oxford: Clarendon Press, 1949. Maps, an index, and a bibliography. A useful and well-written volume that fills a real gap and is of utmost value to both scholars and students. Fuller treatment of peripheral areas would have increased its usefulness.

22 Cook, J. M. *The Greeks in Ionia and the East.* Ancient Peoples and Places, vol. 31. N. Y.: Praeger, 1963. A list of illustrations, 75 photographs, 46 line drawings, 7 maps, a chronological table, bibliography, notes on the plates, and an index. A worthy addition to an excellent series, intended for the layman, written with clarity and mastery of its subject.

23 Cousinéry, Esprit Marie. *Voyage dans la Macédoine, Contenant des Recherches sur l'Histoire, la Géographie et les Antiquités de ce Pays.* 2 vols. bound in 1. Paris: Imprimerie Royale, 1831. Many notes, catalogs of coins and medals, plates, many texts of inscriptions, but no bibliography or index. The author was a French diplomat and traveller. Although his reputation was that of being a learned man, this work lacks distinction and is also much out-of-date.

24 Cox, George W[illiam]. *A General History of Greece. From the Earliest Period to the Death of Alexander the Great. With a Sketch of the Subsequent History to the Present Time.* N. Y.: Harper and Brothers, 1876. An expanded table of contents with chronological guides, maps with a listing for them, a list of the Latin forms of Greek names, margin notes, footnotes, a chronological table from 670 B.C. to 1862 A.D., and an index. A remarkable volume to be recommended to the general reader; now sadly out-of-date.

25 Daremberg, Charles Victor and Saglio, Edmond. *Dictionnaire des Antiquités Grecques et Romaines d'après les Textes et les Monuments.* In 53 fascicles. Paris: Hachette, 1873-1919. 5 vols. in 10 by the same publisher in 1877–1919. 5 vols. in 12 by the same publisher in 1881. A work of the highest authority with long, signed articles by specialists with very detailed bibliographies. Indexes of authors, Greek words, Latin words, and subjects are included.

26 Delbrück, Hans. *Geschichte der Kriegskunst im Rahmen der Politischen Geschichte.* 4 vols. Berlin: Georg Stilke, 1900-20. Berlin: W. de Gruyter, c1962-64. The 1962-64 set is a photo-reproduction of the first edition. Contains many footnotes, maps, diagrams, and an index to the set in the last volume. A work that contains much that is interesting and important. It was written with vigor and industry. Printed in the Old German type.

27 Dittenberger, Wilhelm. *Orientis Graeci Inscriptiones Selectae. Supplementum Sylloges Inscriptionum Graecarum.* 2 vols. Lipsiae: S. Hirzel, 1903-05. Hildesheim: Georg Olms, 1960. The 1960 edition is a photoreproduction of the original. Contains a table of contents in each volume, *many* footnotes, indexes of Greek names, a listing of periodical articles by journal name, and the inscriptions with notes. A supplement to his *Sylloge Inscriptionum Graecarum.* Contains selections of Greek inscriptions of the East. An extremely useful work of high quality, and well assembled.

28 ———. *Sylloge Inscriptionum Graecarum.* 2 vols. Lipsiae: S. Hirzel, 1883. Later editions by the same publisher in 1898-1901 (in 3 vols.) and in 1915-24 (as 4 vols. in 5). The last edition was photoreproduced in 1960. The texts of inscriptions with commentary. The 1915 edition contains various indices and a table of corresponding numbers in the first edition and in other similar collections. A very useful collection of Greek inscriptions of historical significance.

29 Ehrenberg, Victor. *Aspects of the Ancient World; Essays and Reviews.* Oxford: Alden Press; N. Y.: W. Salloch, 1946. Many footnotes, plates and an index. A collection of articles written by Ehrenberg between 1926 and 1945, many of which originally

appeared in journals not well known in America. The contents
reflect much careful scholarship and their range is impressive.

30 Engelmann, Wilhelm. *Bibliotheca Scriptorum Classicorum et
Graecorum et Latinorum. Alphabetisches Verzeichniss der
Ausgaben, uebersetzungen und Erläuterungsschriften der Greich-
ischen und Lateinischen Schriftsteller, Welche vom Jahre 1700
bis zu Ende des Jahres 1846 Besonders in Deutschland Gedruckt
Worden Sind.* 2 vols. 6th. ed. Leipzig: W. Engelmann, 1847.
7th. ed. by the same publisher in 1858, and an 8th. in 1880-82.
Hildesheim: Georg Olms, 1959. The first five editions were
compiled by T. C. F. Enslin. The fifth, edited by C. W. Lofland,
was reissued with a supplement in 1840 by W. Engelmann.
A supplement was published in 1853 by Engelmann with the title:
*Supplement-Heft: Enthaltend die Literatur von anfang des Jahres
1847 bis Ende 1852.* The standard bibliography for the period,
especially useful for information about editions and translations.
Continued by Klussmann's bibliography.

31 Ferguson, William Scott. *Greek Imperialism.* Boston and N. Y.:
Houghton Mifflin, 1913. A collection of 7 lectures, 6 of which
were delivered at the Lowell Institute during February, 1913.
Contains notes, a select bibliography at the end of each lecture,
and an index. A well-organized and compelling, popular study
written in an individual, vigorous and impressive style. Because of
the author's wide knowledge of inscriptions and ancient literature
and his skillful judgment, he is to be ranked at the forefront
of English-writing scholars in the field of Greek history.

32 Freeman, Edward A. *Historical Essays.* 2d. ser. London and N. Y.:
Macmillan, 1873. Later editions by the same publisher in 1880
and 1889. A collection of essays—all but the first written as
reviews—reprinted from the original sources with appropriate
revisions and simplifications and improvement of style.

33 Göttling, C. W. *Gesammelte Abhandlungen aus dem Classischen
Alterthume.* 2 vols. Vol. 1: Halle: Verlag der Buchhandlung
des Waisenhauses, 1851. Vol. 2: München: Friedrich Bruckmann's
Verlag, 1863. A table of contents in each volume, notes, fold-out
plates, diagrams, and an index for the set in vol. 2. A well-written

volume by an eminent philologist who studied all areas of antiquity.

34 Grégoriadis, N. *L'Art de la Guerre d'Homère à Alexandre le Grand.* Collection de l'Institut Français d'Athènes, 55. Athènes, 1951. Table of contents and notes. A useful work by a professional military man.

35 Grote, George. *History of Greece.* 12 vols. London: J. Murray, 1846-56. Later editions by the same publisher in 1862 (in 8 vols.), 1870 (in 12 vols.), 1872 (in 10 vols.), and 1888 (in 10 vols.). The following American editions were published: Boston: J. P. Jewett and Co., 1851-57 (vol. 9-12, N. Y.: Harper and Brothers, 1853-57); N. Y.: Harper and Brothers; [Boston]: J. P. Jewett and Co., 1851-67; N. Y.: Harper and Brothers, 1853-72; N. Y.: E. P. Dutton and Co.; London: J. M. Dent and Co., [1906]. Many footnotes, maps, an extensive index in the last volume for the set, and an expanded table of contents in each volume. Once a standard work, now superseded, it was translated into many languages and revised up to 1907. The set is by a scholar of international reputation, known for his thoroughness of scholarship, and it contains an enormous amount of scholarly detail which tends to make the narrative tedious.

36 Hammond, N. G. L. *History of Greece to 322 B.C.* Oxford: Clarendon Press, 1959. 2d. ed. by the same publisher in 1967. Plates and diagrams, good maps, notes, an index, and a set of appendices which present the author's arguments on disputed points. An able scholar's view of Greek history which is interesting, valuable, and useful as a handbook. The volume portrays the author's sound judgment and his carefully and clearly argued presentation.

37 Hatzfeld, Jean. *Histoire de la Grèce Ancienne.* Paris: Payot, 1950. Tr. by A. C. Harrison and E. H. Goddard as *History of Ancient Greece.* London: Oliver and Boyd, 1966. First American ed. tr. by A. C. Harrison. Rev. by André Aymard. Ed. by E. H. Goddard. N. Y.: Norton, 1966. A selective bibliography by D. J. Mosley and maps. Mosley made certain editorial changes for the English edition. A history of Greece down to the Roman

invasion by an eminent historian. Emphasis is on the Hellenistic period with due space given to intellectual and social development.

38 Head, Barclay V[incent]. *Historia Numorum; a Manual of Greek Numismatics*. Oxford: Clarendon Press, 1887. New enl. ed. by B. V. Head, assisted by G. F. Hill, George Macdonald, and W. Wroth. Oxford: Clarendon Press, 1911. A table of contents, a table of measurements, table of weights, plates of alphabets, plates of coins, the following indexes: geographical, kings and dynasts, remarkable inscriptions, engravers' names, and subjects, and a bibliography. A listing of coins by place and including word descriptions. A monumental work which brings together a great mass of material and makes it useful.

39 Hicks, E[dward] L[ee]. *A Manual of Greek Historical Inscriptions*. Oxford: Clarendon Press, 1882. New and rev. ed. with G. F. Hill printed by the same publisher in 1901. A table of contents, an index, but no bibliography. A chronological presentation of inscriptions from 700 B.C. to 80 B.C. with commentary. An excellent and instructive volume.

40 Höistad, Ragnar. *Cynic Hero and Cynic King; Studies in the Cynic Conception of Man*. Uppsala: [Carl Bloms Boktryckeri], 1948. A table of contents, one plate, notes, bibliography, and a name and subject index. A complete review of the principal theses and critical problems in the analysis of mythological heroes. An excellent example of the use of historical method.

41 Hoffmann, Sam. Frider. Guil. *Bibliographisches Lexicon der Gesammten Literatur der Griechen*. 3 vols. Leipzig: Neudruck der Ausgabe, 1838. Reprinted in Amsterdam: Verlag Adolf M. Hakkert, 1961. An alphabetical listing of sources which contains a chronological listing of editions.

42 Holdich, Sir Thomas [Hungerford]. *Gates of India, Being an Historical Narrative*. London: Macmillan, 1910. Table of contents, maps, few notes, index. A picturesque narrative intended for the statesman and not the historian; not a book of reference. A review by G. M. Bolling notes the shocking inaccuracy of the spelling of proper names.

43 Holm, Adolf. *Griechische Geschichte von Ihrem Ursprunge bis zum Untergange der Selbstandigkeit des Griechischen Volkes.* 4 vols. Berlin: Calvary, 1893. Tr. by the publisher as *History of Greece from its Commencement to the Close of the Greek Nation.* 4 vols. N. Y. and London: Macmillan, 1894-98. Reprinted by the same published in 1898-1900. Notes at the end of each chapter which contain valuable criticisms of sources, and an index to the set in the last volume. A sensible and interesting work that displays the author's power to bring out characteristic features and his awareness of the latest literature in all languages. The narrative is excellent as is the translation.

44 Imhoof-Blumer, F[riedrich]. *Monnaies Grecques.* Paris: C. Rollin et Feuardent, 1883. Leipzig: K. F. Koehler's Antiquarium, 1883. A table of contents, notes, plates and illustrations, a short bibliography, and various indexes—person and place, coin type, symbols and remarkable attributes, legends and inscriptions, and Greek words. An extensive listing of coins with notes and comments. Neither a history of Greek money nor a manual of numismatics, but a selection of coins; a most important work.

45 ————. *Porträtköpfe auf Antiken Münzen Hellenischer und Hellenisierter Völker.* Leipzig: B. G. Teubner, 1885. A table of contents, notes, plates, and indexes—people, land and state, kind, person. A listing of portraits by place with word descriptions. A volume of interest to archaeologists, philologists, historians, and students.

46 Instinsky, Hans Ulrich. "Mensch und Gott in der Geschichte," *Beiträge zur Geistigen Überlieferung* (Godesberg: Verlag Helmut Küpper, 1947), 184-224. Many notes but no index or bibliography.

47 Jacoby, Felix. *Die Fragmente der Griechischen Historiker.* 4 vols. Berlin: Weidmann, 1923-1930. 3 vols. in 15. Leiden: E. J. Brill, 1957-58. The text of the fragments, their translation into German, and a learned and valuable commentary. There is also an index for this and the Müller set. A comprehensive collection of nearly all fragments to which the set pertains. A great undertaking by one of the strong personalities in the world of scholarship, the set furnishes a trustworthy standard to check attributions of authorship. The set reflects enormous learning, a mastery of the

material, and an astonishing perseverance in tracking down every detail.

48 Jones, A. H. M. *The Greek City from Alexander to Justinian.* Oxford: Clarendon Press, 1940. Many notes, a list of useful books and articles, a geographical index, an index of sovereigns, a subject index, and an index of Greek words. A discussion of the development of the Greek city under the rule of kings and the role they played in the Hellenistic world. A well-planned, well-presented volume written in a fluent and lucid style. A companion volume to the author's *Cities of the Eastern Roman Provinces* (1937), this volume contains views which are stimulating and worth considering. In a review, Rostovtzeff called this work ". . . a fine contribution to our knowledge."

49 Kaerst, Julius. *Studien zur Entwichlung und Theoretischen Begründung der Monarchie im Altertum.* Historische Bibliothek, VI. Munich und Leipzig: K. Oldenbourg, 1898. Printed in the old German type, with a table of contents and many notes. A valuable work by a noted scholar.

50 Kern, Otto. *Die Religion der Griechen.* 3 vols. Berlin: Weidmannsche Buchhandlung, 1926-38. A table of contents, an index in the first volume and one for the set in the last, a chronology for 777/6 B.C. to 529 A.D., a Greek word index, and many notes. An excellent volume which is not too technical. The only need is for more attention to be paid to non-German literature.

51 Klussmann, Rudolf. *Bibliotheca Scriptorum Classicorum et Graecorum et Latinorum. Die Literatur von 1878 bis 1896 einschliesslich umfassend.* 2 vols. in 4. Leipzig: O. R. Reisland, 1909-13. An excellent bibliography which was also published as volumes 146, 151, 156, and 165 of the *Jahresbericht über die Fortschritte der Klassischen Altertumswissenschaft* (Berlin, 1909 to 1913). A supplement to Engelmann's bibliography.

52 Kromayer, Johannes. *Antike Schlachtfelder in Griechenland. Baust eine zu einer Antiken Kriegsgeschichte.* 4 vols. in 5. Berlin: Weidmannsche Buchhandlung, 1903-31. An expanded table of contents, fold-out maps in each volume, notes, a bibliography, tables, a chronology from 490-31 B.C., a list of places with

references to the maps, and a list of sources with each section. An important work based on an expedition to Greece made in 1900. Written from a military point of view, it equates the military operations of antiquity with modern strategy and tactics.

53 Kromayer, Johannes and Veith, Georg. *Heerwesen und Kriegfuhrung der Griechen und Romer.* Handbuch der Altertumswissenschaft, Section 4, pt. 3, vol. 2. Munich: C. H. Beck, 1928. Many plates, diagrams, notes and maps; a brief bibliography is given before each section. Part of a series edited by Walter Otto designed to replace the *Handbuch* of Ivan Müller. An excellent volume dealing with military history as well as strategy and armament.

54 Laistner, M. L. W. *A History of the Greek World from 497 to 323 B.C.* London: Methuen, 1936. 2d. ed. by the same publisher in 1947. 3d. ed. N. Y.: Barnes and Noble, 1962. Notes, 4 maps, a selected bibliography, an index, and sources and authorities for the period covered. Written soberly, critically, and with scholarly competence, but without enthusiasm. Political and military history are emphasized.

55 Lambrino, Scarlat. *Bibliographie de l'Antiquité Classique, 1896-1914.* Paris: Société d'Edition "Les Belles Lettres," 1951- . The first volume was reprinted by the same company in 1961. Lists editions, translations, and works about classical writers in books and journals. Part one is "Auteurs et Textes." The set covers all phases of Greco-Latin antiquity and was continued by Marouzeau's bibliography.

56 Lassen, Christian. *Indische Alterthumskunde.* 4 vols. Bonn and Leipzig: H. B. Koenig, 1847-62. London: Williams and Norgate, 1867-74. Published as 5 vols. in Leipzig: L. A. Kittler, 1858-74. An expanded table of contents in each volume, notes, and fold-out maps. A scholarly set regrettably lacking an index and bibliography.

57 Launey, Marcel. *Recherches sur les Armées Hellénistiques.* 2 vols. Bibliothèque des Écoles Françaises d'Athènes et de Rome, No. 169. Paris: E. de Boccard, 1949-50. Many notes, a general index, a list of principal abbreviations, and a "Plan de la Prosopographie" and its index. The volume aims at a complete collection of evidence

in the study of the army as an element in the society of the
Hellenistic world. Every fact was weighed for its own sake before
inclusion. The scope of treatment is unequalled in any other work.

58 L'Orange, H. P. *Apotheosis in Ancient Portraiture.* Cambridge,
Mass.: Harvard University Press, 1947. A table of contents, notes,
an index, and 97 figures in the text. A very useful volume.

59 Mahaffy, John Pentland. *Greek Life and Thought from the Death of
Alexander to the Roman Conquest.* N. Y. and London:
Macmillan, 1887. 2d. ed., corrected and considerably enlarged
by the same company in 1896. A chronological table, an index,
and a discussion of fragments in the appendix. An important
work in Hellenistic history by a man who did much to give the
subject a status of its own in classical studies. A review in the
American Journal of Philology calls this a bright and suggestive
book but one not to be taken in "dead earnest" because of the
need to verify and evaluate parallels drawn between ancient and
modern history. The review warns that the real thesis of the
volume is ". . . the miserable narrowness of English scholarship
and the unreason of Home Rule."

60 ———. *Problems in Greek History.* N. Y. and London: Macmillan,
1892. A detailed table of contents, a list of works by the author,
subject guides in the margins, and many notes. The author is
just in his intuitive appreciation of historical perspective and
recognizes the continuity of history. His estimate of Alexander
as neither a butcher nor a demigod makes the volume helpful
even to the specialist and of particular interest and value for the
modern Hellenist.

*61 Mallet, Domenique. *Les Rapports des Grecques avec l'Egypte.*
Cairo: Imprimerie de l'Institut Français d'Archéologie Orientale,
1922. The University of Michigan copy is "missing."

62 Marouzeau, Jules. *Dix Années de Bibliographie Classique;
Bibliographie Critique et Analytique de l'Antiquité Gréco-
Latine pour la Période 1914-1924.* 2 vols. Paris: Société d'Edition
"Les Belles Lettres," 1927-28. Vol. 1 is "Auteurs et Textes";

---

* Those materials which were unavailable for examination are preceded by an
asterisk. Availability for titles was checked through the Library of Congress
in Washington, D.C.

Vol. 2 is "Matieres et Disciplines." An excellent bibliography whose subject volume includes the whole field of history and culture of the classical world. Continued by *l'Année Philologique*.

63 Mionnet, T. E. *Descriptione de Médailles Antiques, Grecques et Romaines*; *Avec leur Degré de Rareté et Leur Estimation*; *Ouvrage Servant de Catalogue à une Suite de Plus de Vint Mille Empreintes en Soufre, Prises sur les Pièces Originales*. 7 vols. Paris: Imprimerie de Testu, 1806-13. Suppl. published in 9 vols. Paris: Testu: (vol. 2-9 say Paris: Chez l'Auteur), 1819-37. Each volume contains a list of names covered in that volume.

64 Müller, Karl and Müller, Theodor. *Fragmenta Historicum Graecorum*. 5 vols. Paris: Editore Ambrosio Firmin Didot, 1883-85. A table of contents, notes, Greek-word index, French index, and reproductions of inscriptions. A valuable collection of the texts of existing fragments of lost Greek historical works. It has been replaced by Jacoby's *Fragmente der Griechischen Historiker*.

65 Nachmanson, Ernst. *Historische Griechische Inschriften bis auf Alexander den Grossen*. Kleine Texte für Vorlesungen und Übungen (Herausgegeben von Hans Lietzmann), nr. 121. Bonn: Marcus and E. Weber's Verlag, 1913. A table of contents, a list of abbreviations, indexes, many notes, and Greek inscriptions with comments.

66 Niebuhr, B[artold] G[eorg]. *Historische und Philologische Vorträge*. 4 vols. Berlin: G. Reimer, 1846-58. Printed in the old German type, with an expanded table of contents in each volume, several extensive indexes, and a few notes. A scholarly title by an historian noted for his critical treatment of literary sources.

*67 Noeldeke, Theodor. *Persische Studien*. 2 vols. Wien: F. Tempsky, 1888-92. Located in the United States at the Library of Congress (too brittle to loan) and at the New Jersey Public Library (non-circulating).

68 Olmstead, A. T. *History of the Persian Empire*. [*Achaemenid Period*]. Chicago: University of Chicago Press, 1948. A paperbound

edition is available from the same publisher as the first Phoenix ed., [1959 (c1948)]. Notes, fine plates, maps, a topographical index, name index, and a subject index. A companion and sequal to his *History of Assyria* (1923) and *History of Syria and Palestine* (1931). A combination of all the diverse materials concerning almost every aspect of ancient civilizations with copious quotations from ancient sources. However, E. J. Bikerman criticized the volume because there is no cross reference between text and illustrations, the narrative lacks continuity, and the author conceals uncertainties in our knowledge.

69 Olsen, Ørjan [Mikael]. *La Conquête de la Terre; Histoire des Découvertes et des Explorations depuis les Origines Jusqu'à Nos Jours.* Tr. from Norwegian by E. Guerre. 6 vols. Paris: Payot, 1933. Table of contents, illustrations, maps, but no notes. A well-written popular account by a noted explorer; contains much that is new and interesting.

70 *Oxford Classical Dictionary*, ed. by M. Cary, A.D. Nock, [and others]. Oxford: Clarendon Press, 1949. A scholarly dictionary with signed articles, mostly brief, but there are also longer survey articles. Bibliographies are limited to a few of the best works on the subject in English and foreign languages.

71 Paparrēghopoulos, Kōnstantinos. *Historia. Tou Hellenikou Ethnous apo tōn Archaiotatōn Chronōn Mechri tōn Kath'hēmas.* 5 vols. and atlas. Athens, 1860-77. Tr. into French as *Histoire de la Nation Héllenique.* 5 vols. and atlas. Paris, 1885-87 and as 2 vols. in 1902. Table of contents and an index, but no notes. This work is still read as a classic by Greeks. The author displays judicious discrimination and an originality and independence of judgment.

72 Pauly, August Friedrich von and Wissowa, Georg. *Der Kleine Pauly: Lexikon der Antike, auf der Grundlage von Paulys Realencyclopadie der Classischen Altertumswissenschaft unter Mitwirkung Zahlreicher Fachgelehrter, bearb. und hrsg. von Konrat Ziegler und Walther Sontheimer.* Stuttgart: Alfred Druckenmüller Verlag, 1964- . An abridgement of *Paulys Real-Encyclopadie* with its articles in concise form; bibliographical references have been updated.

73 ———. *Paulys Real-Encyclopädie der Classischen Altertumswissenschaft.* Stuttgart: J. B. Metzlerscher Verlag, 1894-1962, with supplements still being published. The standard, scholarly work on all aspects of antiquity with long, signed articles by specialists. Includes extensive bibliographies.

74 Peck, Harry Thurston, ed. *Harper's Dictionary of Classical Literature and Antiquities.* N. Y.: Harper, 1897. Another edition was published by the same company in 1898. N. Y.: American Book Co., [1937? c1923]. A scholarly work with concise articles, brief bibliographies, and good illustrations.

75 Pöhlmann, Robert v. *Griechische Geschichte und Quellenkunde.* Handbuch der Klassischen Altertumswissenschaft, III 4. Munich: C. H. Beck, 1889. A later edition was published by the same company in 1914. A table of contents, notes, and an index, but no bibliography, which is unfortunate because of the extensive listing of sources in the text. A clever but modernistic outline of Greek social conditions and ideas by a well-known German historian.

76 Prentice, William Kelly. *The Ancient Greeks; Studies Toward a Better Understanding of the Ancient World.* Princeton: Princeton University Press; London: H. Milford, Oxford University Press, 1940. Many footnotes and an index, but no bibliography. An interpretation based on 40 years study and teaching. A scholarly and readable volume, intensely interesting as well as provocative.

77 Rawlinson, Hugh George. *Intercourse of India and the Western World from the Earliest Times to the Fall of Rome.* Cambridge: University Press, 1916. 2d ed. by the same publisher in 1926. Illustrations, a map, a bibliography, an index, notes, and a list of rulers in the area down to 474 A.D., this is an interesting, fully documented volume that fills a long-felt need. The illustrations are excellent, but the volume was written for the scholar only.

78 *Reallexikon für Antike und Christentum.* Stuttgart: Hiersemann, 1950-1964. (Still being published). A standard work containing long, signed articles with extensive bibliographies dealing with the relationship of the ancient world to Christianity up to the sixth century A.D.

79 Rostovtzeff, Mikhail Ivanovich. *Ocherk Istorīi Drevniāgo Mīra*:
   Bostok'-Gretsiia Pim'. Berlin: Knigoizdatel'stvo "Slovo," 1924.
   Tr. from the Russian by J. D. Duff as *History of the Ancient*
   World. 2 vols. Oxford: Clarendon Press, 1926-45. Many plates,
   maps, an index, chronology, and a bibliography. The first volume
   concerns "The Orient and Greece"; the second "Rome."
   A standard work which reflects excellent planning. Its weakest
   side is geography, and the translation is not always the best.
   It can be recommended to students as a sound and readable survey
   of the history of the countries with which it deals.

80 Schlegel, Fried. v. *Fried. v. Schlegel's Sämtliche Werke*. 10 vols.
   Wein: I. Klang, 1822-25. 2d. enl. ed. in 15 vols. by the same
   publisher in 1846. A table of contents in each volume and a few
   notes, but no index or bibliography. A valuable set, printed in the
   old German type, by a well-known German literary historian
   and critic.

81 Schlosser, Friedrich Christoph. *F. C. Schlosser's Weltgeschichte*
   für das Deutsche Volk. 19 vols. Berlin: O. Seehagen, 1844-57.
   A table of contents, and vol. 19 is the index to the set, but there are
   no notes. This remarkable work would have been of much
   greater value had it been documented.

82 Schneider, Carl. *Kulturgeschichte des Hellenismus*. Munich:
   Beck, [1967]- . An expanded table of contents, a long list of
   abbreviations, and notes. A scholarly title which is still being
   published.

83 Smith, Vincent A. *Early History of India from 600 B.C. to the*
   Muhammadon Conquest, Including the Invasion of Alexander
   the Great. Oxford: Clarendon Press, 1904. Later editions by the
   same publisher in 1908, 1914, 1924, and 1957. Illustrations,
   maps and plans, many notes, an index, but no bibliography.
   This is a comprehensive survey by one whose knowledge of India
   and eminence as a numismatist and archaeologist make this an
   admirable handbook.

84 Smith, Sir William. *Dictionary of Greek and Roman Biography*
   and Mythology. 3 vols. London: Taylor and Walton, 1844-49.
   Boston: Little and Brown, 1849. London: J. Murray, 1876.
   A later edition was published by the same company in 1890.

A standard work, now much out-of-date, containing long signed articles and bibliographies of the best non-classical sources.

85 Spiegel, Friedrich von. *Erânische Altertumskunde*. 3 vols. Leipzig: W. Engelmann, 1871-78. An expanded table of contents in each volume and many notes, but no bibliography. A scholarly and valuable title.

86 Sykes, Sir Percey. *A History of Persia*. 2 vols. London: Macmillan, 1915. Later editions by the same company in 1921 and 1930, and the 3d. ed. was reprinted in N. Y.: St. Martins; London: Macmillan, 1958. Maps, illustrations, many notes, a list of authorities, and an index in the second volume. An attempt to focus all that is known of the ancient empires in their relations with Persia. An admirable piece of work, always delightful, because of the author's personal knowledge of the area. The illustrations deserve special notice for their abundance and clarity.

87 Thomson, James Oliver. *History of Ancient Geography*. Cambridge: University Press, 1948. Reprinted in N. Y.: Biblo and Tannen, 1965. Many illustrations, maps, diagrams, many notes, a short and systematic bibliography, and an index. The volume is eminently readable and contains a mass of detail and copious notes. A thorough, fully documented investigation of a difficult subject.

88 Tod, Marcus N., ed. *A Selection of Greek Historical Inscriptions*. 2 vols. Oxford: Clarendon Press, 1933-48. Reprinted by the same publisher in 1951-51. A list of Athenian Eponymous Archons from 403 to 323 B.C., a table of concordance, a proper name index, a subject index, and an index of Greek words and phrases. A standard work listing inscriptions from the fifth century to 323 B.C. It also includes a history, description, and bibliography for each stone. This triple *lemmata* makes the set indispensable to the student of Greek history.

89 Tozer, Henry Fanshawe. *A History of Ancient Geography*. Cambridge: University Press, 1897. 2d. ed. with additional notes by M. Cary by the same publisher in 1935. N. Y.: Biblo and Tannen, 1964. Maps, notes, an index, and subject guides in the margin. The second edition has a select bibliography. This set does not supersede Bunbury's monumental work, but it serves as an

introduction to it. A concise and interesting history of geography in English and a much-needed work.

90 Van Sickle, Clifton Edwin. *A Political and Cultural History of the Ancient World from Prehistoric Times to the Dissolution of the Roman Empire in the West*. 2 vols. Boston: Houghton Mifflin, 1947-48. A table of contents, maps on the endpapers, illustrations, a few notes, an index, and a selected bibliography. Written for the college undergraduate, it is clear and concise. The author seems to be more interested in facts than in concepts and a number of serious mistakes in judgment have been noted by T. S. Brown. However, Brown judged it to be among the best available in the field.

91 Visconti, Ennio Quirino. *Iconographie Grecque*. 2 vols. in 3. Paris: Impr. de P. Didot l'aîne, 1808. Later published in Italy as *Iconographie Grecque*; *ou, Recueil des Portraits Authentiques des Empereurs, Rois, et Hommes Illustres de l'Antiquité*. 3 vols. Milan: J. P. Giegler, 1824-26. An expanded table of contents in each volume, plates and a listing of them in each volume, and notes. A valuable and scholarly volume.

92 Wachsmuth, Curt. *Einleitung in das Studium der Alten Geschichte*. Leipzig: S. Hirzel, 1895. An expanded table of contents, notes, and an index. An excellent volume of value to the scholar by one who knows his subject well.

93 Wendland, Paul. *Die Hellenistisch-Römische Kultur in Ihren Beziehungen zu Judentum und Christentum*. Handbuch zum Neuen Testament, Bd. I, Teil 2. Tubingen: J. C. B. Mohr (Paul Siebeck), 1907. Later edition by the same publisher in 1912. A table of contents, notes, illustrations, and a bibliography before each section. A highly recommended and most useful volume.

94 Wilcken, Ulrich. *Griechische Geschichte im Rahmen der Altertumsgeschichte*. Berlin and Munich: R. Oldenbourg, 1924. Later editions by the same publisher in 1926, 1931, 1939, 1943, 1948, 1951, 1958, and 1962. A table of contents, illustrations, notes which are collected at the end, a parallel chronology for Greek and Oriental history from 2850 to 30 B.C., 2 fold-out maps, and a bibliographical essay. A sketch of Greek history designed

primarily as a textbook for use in schools. An excellent, clearly written work, but the lack of an index is conspicuous.

95 ———. *Über Werden und Vergehen der Universalreiche*. Bonn: Verlag von Friedrich Cohen, 1915. A useful volume by a noted scholar. It would have been more useful had the notes been with the text rather than collected at the end.

96 Zell, Karl. *Ferienschriften*. 3 vols. Freiburg im Breisgau: Fried. Wagner, 1826-33. A table of contents and notes at the end of each chapter. The set is printed in the old German type.

II. Classical Sources

1 Agis of Argos (?). [*Alexanderepos.*] Fragments-Jacoby.

2 Amyntas. *Stages in Asia.* Fragments-Jacoby.

3 Amyntianos. *To Alexander.* Fragments-Jacoby.

4 Anaximenes of Lampsacus. *History of Alexander.* Fragments-Jacoby.

5 Androsthenes. No title. Fragments-Jacoby.

6 Antidamas of Hierakleopolis. *History of Alexander of Macedon.* Fragments-Jacoby.

7 Antikleides of Athens. *On Alexander.* Fragments-Jacoby.

8 Antigonus of Carystus. *Lives of Philosophers.* Fragments-Jacoby.

9 Apion of Oasis and Alexandria. *In Praise of King Alexander.* Fragments-Jacoby.

10 Archelaus of Cappadocia. No title. Fragments-Jacoby.

11 Aristobulus of Cassandreia. *History of Alexander.* Fragments-Jacoby.

12 Aristos of Salamis (Kypros). *History of Alexander.* Fragments-Jacoby.

13 Aristotle. *Alexander* or *On Colonisation.* Fragments-*The Works of Aristotle*, translated into English under the editorship of Sir David Ross. Vol. 12 "Select Fragments." Oxford: At the Clarendon Press, 1952.

When only fragments of the work remain and these fragments have been collected by Felix Jacoby, the words "Fragments-Jacoby" will be used.

14 Arrianus, Flavius. *Anabasis Alexandri* and the *Indica*. There are
   many translations of these works (usually bound together)
   in many languages. A well-known example is part of the Loeb
   Classical Library: *Arrian*, with an English translation by Iliff
   Robson .... London: W. Heinemann, Ltd.; N. Y.: G. P. Putnam's
   Sons, 1929-33.

15 Asclepiades. No title. Fragments-Jacoby. Also collected in
   The Greek Anthology, edited by A.S.F. Gow and D. L. Page.
   4 vols. Cambridge: At the University Press, 1965-68.

16 Baiton. *Stages in Alexander's Journey*. Fragments-Jacoby.

17 Berossos (Berosus) of Marduk. *History of Babylonia*.
   Fragments-Jacoby.

18 Callisthenes. *Alexander's Deeds*. Fragments-Jacoby.

19 ————. *Hellenica*. Fragments-Jacoby.

20 ————. *History of Greece*. Fragments-Jacoby.

21 Chares of Mitylene. *History of Alexander*. Fragments-Jacoby.

22 Choerilus of Iasos. No title. Fragments-Jacoby.

23 Cleitarchus of Alexandria. *History of Alexander*. 12 books.
   Fragments-Jacoby.

24 Curtius Rufus, Quintus. *History of Alexander*. There are many
   translations of this work in many languages. A well-known example
   is part of the Loeb Classical Library: *Quintus Curtius*, with an
   English translation by John C. Rolfe. Cambridge, Mass.:
   Harvard University Press, 1946.

25 Demosthenes. *On the Treaties with Alexander*. There are many
   translations of this work in many languages. A well-known example
   is part of the Loeb Classical Library: *Demosthenes: Olynthiacs,
   Philippics, Minor Public Speeches, Speech Against Leptines*,
   with an English translation by J. H. Vince. London: William
   Heinemann, Ltd.; N. Y.: G. P. Putnam's Sons, 1930.

26 Diodorus Siculus. *Bibliotheca Historica*. There are many translations
   of this work in many languages. A well-known example is part
   of the Loeb Classical Library: *Diodorus of Sicily*, with an English

translation by C. H. Oldfather. 12 vols. London: W. Heinemann, Ltd.; N. Y.: G. P. Punam's Sons, 1933-67.

27 Diognetos (of Erythrai?). No title. Fragments-Jacoby.

28 Dorotheos of Athens. *History of Alexander*. Fragments-Jacoby.

29 Eumenes of Cardia and Diotus of Erythrae, comp. *Ephemerides*. Fragments-Jacoby.

30 Ephippos of Olynthus. *On the Death of Alexander and Hephaestion*. Fragments-Jacoby.

31 Hegesias of Magnesia (Sipylos). *History of Alexander*. Fragments-Jacoby.

32 Hieronymus of Cardia. No title. Fragments-Jacoby.

33 Justinus, Marcus Junianus. *Philippic History*. There are many editions of this work in many languages. An example in English is: *The Historie of Iustine.* . . . London: Printed by William Iaggard, 1606.

34 Kyrsilos of Pharsalos. No title. Fragments-Jacoby.

35 Leon of Byzantium. *The Deeds of Alexander*. Fragments-Jacoby.

36 Manetho of Sebennytos. *Aegyptiaca*. Fragments-C. Müller. *Fragmenta Historicum Graecorum*. Paris, 1841-70.

37 Marsyas of Pella. *History of Attica*. 12 books. Fragments-Jacoby.

38 ———. *History of Macedon*. 10 books. Fragments-Jacoby.

39 ———. *The Training of Alexander*. Fragments-Jacoby.

40 Medeios (Medius) of Larissa. No title. Fragments-Jacoby.

41 Megasthenes. *Indika*. Fragments-Jacoby.

42 Menaichmos of Sikyon. *On the Macedonian Alexander*. Fragments-Jacoby.

43 Nearchus of Crete. *Circumnavigation of India* (?). Fragments-Jacoby. Arrian's *Indica* is based on the writings of Nearchus (see above).

44 Nikanor. *Life of Alexander*. Fragments-Jacoby.

45 Nikobule. No title. Fragments-Jacoby.

46 Nymphis. No title. Fragments-Jacoby.

47 Onescritus of Astypaloea. *Education of Alexander.* Fragments-Jacoby.

48 Philochorus of Anaphlystus. *Atthis.* Fragments-Jacoby.

49 Philonides of Crete. No title. Fragments-Jacoby.

50 Plutarch. *Lives of the Noble Grecians and Romans.* There are many translations of this work. A well-known example is part of the Loeb Classical Library: *Plutarch's Lives,* with an English translation by Bernadotte Perrin. 11 vols. London: W. Heinemann, Ltd.; N. Y.: Macmillan, 1914-26.

51 ———. *Moralia.* 14 vols. Vol. 4 "On the Fortune or the Virtue of Alexander." There are many translatons of this work. A well-known example is part of the Loeb Classical Library: *Moralia,* with the English translation by Frank Cole Babbitt. Cambridge: Harvard University Press, 1936.

52 Polyaenus. *Strategemata.* There are many versions of this work. One such is entitled *Polyaeni Strategematum Libri Octo.* Batavia: Apud Johannem du Vivie and Jordanum Luchtmans, 1690.

53 Polykleitos of Larissa. *History.* Fragments-Jacoby.

54 Potamon of Mytilene. *On Alexander of Macedon.* Fragments-Jacoby.

55 Ptolemy, Son of Lagus. No title. Fragments-Jacoby.

56 Soterichos of (Thasos?). *Alexanderepos.* Fragments-Jacoby.

57 Strattis of Olynthus. *On the Death of Alexander.* Fragments-Jacoby.

58 ———. *On the Ephemerides of Alexander.* Fragments-Jacoby.

59 Theopompos of Chios. *'Egkō'mion 'Alexàndrou.* Fragments-Jacoby.

60 Varro, Marcus Terentius. *Hebdomades vel de Imaginibus.* Fragments-Jacoby.

III. Pre-Nineteenth Century Materials

*1 Ansaldi, P. "De Profect. Alex. Hieros." Unpublished dissertation, Turin, 1780.

**2 Biedma, Fernando de. *Vida de Alexandro Magno.* Madrid: Imprenta del Reyno, 1634.

*3 Birckhan, M. Joh. Georgius. *Dissertatio Politico-Historica de Alexandro Magno Tyranno.* Lipsiae: Literis Immanuelis Titii, 1706.

4 Botero, Giovanni. *Observations Vpon the Liues of Alexander, Caesar, Scipio.* Newly English. London: Printed by A. Islip, for Iohn Iaggard, 1602.

5 Boulanger, Nicholas Antoine. *Oeuvres de Boulanger.* 8 vols. Paris: Chez J. Serbieres et J.-F. Bastien, 1792-93. Contains an expanded table of contents but no notes.

6 Buache, M. "Recherches Géographiques sur l'Étendue de l'Empire d'Alexandre, et sur les Routes Parcourues par ce Prince dans les Différentes Expéditions. Pour Servir à la Carte de cet Empire, Dressée par feu M. Delisle, pour l'Usage du Roy," *Académie des Sciences. Comptes Rendus,* 1731, 110-23. A fold-out map, margin notes, but no footnotes.

**7 Bury, Richard de. *Histoire de Philippe et d'Alexandre le Grand, Rois de Macédoine.* Paris, 1760.

Those materials which are available in the British Museum, but unavailable in the United States, are preceded by 2 asterisks (**).

Those materials which were unavailable for examination are preceded by an asterisk (*).

8 Caroli, Philippus. "Philippi Caroli Animadversiones Historicae, Philologicae, et Criticae, in Noctes Atlicas Agellii [sic], Q. Curtii Historiam." Unpublished dissertation, Nuremberg, 1663. Edited by Christoph Arnold and published in Nuremberg: Sumtibus M. & J. F. Endterorum, 1663.

*9 Catalanensi, Jacob. *Alexandri Magni Epistola di Situ et Mirabilibus Indiac.* Venetiis, 1499. This title is listed in S. F. G. Hoffmann's *Bibliographisches Lexicon der Gesammten Literatur der Griechen.*

**10 Christina, Queen of Sweden. *The Works of Christina, Queen of Sweden. Containing . . . Reflections on the Life of Alexander the Great.* . . . London: D. Wilson and T. Durham, 1753.

**11 Clarke, Samuel. *The Life and Death of Alexander the Great.* No publisher, 1665.

12 Decembrio, Pier Candido. *Ad Insignem Oratorem Leonardum Aretinum Extracta ex Quadam Epistola Alexandri Magni ad Aristotelem Philosophum 'De Itinere ac Situ Indiae Mirabilia de Responis Arborum Solis et Lunae.'* Bologna: Cod. dell 'Universitaria di Bologna 2387, fol. 60.

**13 Frederick Augustus, Prince of Brunswick-Oels. *Critical Reflections on the Character and Actions of Alexander the Great.* London: Printed for T. Becket and P. A. de Hondt in the Strand, 1767.

14 Freinshemii, Jo. and Lemaire, N. E. *Q. Curtius Rufus ad Codices, Parisinos Recensitus cum Varietate Lectionum de Rebus Alexandri.* Argentorati, 1670. 3 vols. Paris: Colligebat Nicolaus Eligius Lemaire, 1822-24. Maps and notes.

15 Freytag, Frideric Gotthilf. "De Alexandro M. Cornigero." Unpublished dissertation, Academia Lipsiensi, 1715. Lipsiae: Literis Schedianis, 1715. Quotations in Greek and Hebrew; sources cited in the margin; no notes or bibliography.

**16 Gaudenzio, P. *I Fatti d'Alessandro il Grande Spiegati.* No publisher, 1645.

*17 Gronovius, Jacobus. *Arriani Nicomediensis Expeditionis Alexandri Libri Septem*. Batavia: Lugdun, 1707. The copy at Harvard University Library does not circulate.

**18 Guilhelm de Clermont-Lodeve, G. E. J. *Examen Critique des Anciens Historiens d'Alexandre le Grand*. No publisher, 1775. Translated into English as *A Critical Inquiry into the Life of Alexander the Great by the Ancient Historians*. No publisher, 1793.

19 Havercamp, Sigebert. "Dissertationes de Alexandri Magni Numismate: Quoquatuor summa Orbis Terrarum Imperia Continentur ut et de Nummis Contorniatis." Unpublished dissertation, Academiea Lugduno-Batavae, 1722. Published in Batavorum: Janssonios Vanderaa, 1722.

**20 Heckel, J. F. *Dissertatiuncula de Alexandri M. Fortitudine*. No publisher, 1689.

**21 LeLorrain de Vallemont, P. *Dissertation sur une Médaille Singulière d'Alexandre le Grand*. No publisher, 1703.

22 Linquet, Simon-Nicolas-Henri. *Histoire du Siècle d'Alexandre*. Paris: Cellot, 1762. 2d. ed. corr. and enl. by the same publisher in 1769.

23 Mannert, Konrad. *Geschichte der Unmittelbaren Nachfolger Alexanders*. Leipzig: Verlag der Dykischen Buchhandlung, 1787.

24 Manuzio, Aldo. *Alexander Magnus, Epistola de Situ et Mirabilibus Indiae*. Venice: Jac. Catalanensi, 1499.

**25 Matthiae, C. *Historia Alexandri Magni*. No publisher, 1645.

**26 Nicaise, C. *De Nummo Pantheo Hadriani . . . Dissertatio, in qua . . . Instituitur Comparatio inter Hadrianum et Alexandrum M*. No publisher, 1689.

**27 *Observations upon the Liues of Alexander, Caesar, Scipio. Newly Englished [from the Italian of J. B. B.]* No publisher, 1602.

28 Paulini, Andri. *Epistola de Situ Indiae et Itineribus in ea Vastitate ad Aristotelem, Praeceptorem suum Descripta . . . .* Giessae, 1706.

**29 Rodriques de Almada, A. *O Perfeito Heroismo na Preferencia de Julio Cesar à Alexandro Magno.* No publisher, 1762.

**30 Roseo, M. *Vita di Alessandro Magno.* No publisher, 1570.

**31 Saulnier, G. *L'Histoire Entière d'Alexandre le Grand.* No publisher, 1671.

**32 Schlaeger, Carolus Julius. *Commentatio de Numo Alexandri Magni. Acc. De. Thesauro Suppellectilis Antiquariae Sive Collectione Opusculorum Rariorum.* Hamburg: Piscator, 1736. The title is listed in the *British Museum Catalogue.*

**33 *School for Princes; or, Political Reflections upon Three Conspiracies Preceding* [sic] *the Death of Alexander the Great.* Tr. from French by A. O. for Thomas Fabian. London, 1680.

34 Vincent, William. *The Voyage of Nearchus.* London, 1797. Later published as: *Voyage de Nearque, des Bouches de l'Indus Jusqu'à l'Euphrate, ou Journal de la Flotte d'Alexandre . . . .* Paris: de l'Imprimerie de la Republique, 1800.

**35 Virdung, M. M. *Virdungi Alexander Novantiquus sive Magni Gustavi Adolphi . . . cum Alexandro Magno Comparatio.* No publisher, 1633.

**36 Wagner, Andreas. *Dissertatio Historico-Politica de Testamento Alexandri Macedonis.* No publisher, 1709.

**37 Wagner, Joannes (of Breslau). *Virtutes M. Alexandro Poliores.* No publisher, 1670.

**38 Whiston, William. *Of the Thundering Legion . . . as also of Alexander the Great's Meeting the High Priest of the Jews at Jerusalem.* No publisher, 1726.

IV. Modern Sources

A. Monographs

1 Abbott, Jacob. *Histories of Cyrus the Great and Alexander the Great.* Chautauqua Edition. N. Y.: Harper and Bros., 1880. A revision of the 1848 edition with an appendix by Lyman Abbott, and part of Abbott's Illustrated Histories series. Contains a table of contents, maps, illustrations, subject guides at the top of the pages, and notes at the end. Popularized biography.

2 Abel, F. M. *Histoire de la Palestine depuis le Conquête d'Alexandre jusqu'a l'Invasion Arabe.* 2 vols. Paris: Gabalda, 1952. A detailed table of contents, maps, and notes. The author displays a thorough command of sources and a mastery of archaeology, papyri, coins, and inscriptions—a thorough scholarly survey.

3 Abrahams, Israel. *Campaigns in Palestine from Alexander the Great.* London: Published for the British Academy by Humphrey Milford, Oxford University Press, Amen House, 1927. Reprinted in Chicago: Argonaut, 1967. An expanded table of contents, a map, an index, a plate of coins, and a preface by Stanley Cook with notes. A collection of 3 essays which were presented as the Schweich Lectures in 1922.

4 Adcock, F. E. *The Greek and Macedonian Art of War.* Berkeley: University of California Press, 1957. Offered by the same publisher in paperback in 1962. A collection of Sather Foundation lectures with many footnotes, an index, and a discussion of "The Literary Sources." Its mature scholarship and eminent readability make it

Those monographs which were unavailable in the United States are preceded by by an asterisk (*).

a valuable handbook on the art of war for the scholar or the general adult reader.

5 Adler, Maximilianus. "De Alexandri Magni Epistularum Commercio." Unpublished dissertation, Universität Leipzig, 1891. Published in Leipzig: Typis Expressit Oswald Schmidt, 1891. A list of abbreviations, notes, comparisons of texts of Curtius and Arrian and of Plutarch and Arrian, and a vita of the author. Of the literary tradition, the author considers only the administrative acts as authentic, not the private letters.

6 Akurgal, Ekrem. *Die Kunst Anatoliens von Homer bis Alexander.* Berlin: Walter de Gruyter, 1961. Many plates and drawings and a list of illustrations, notes, a name and place index, and a fold-out map. A penetrating study of ancient Anatolian art written mainly for the scholar by an expert in the field.

7 Allcroft, A. H. *The Decline of Hellas: A History of Greece, 362-323 B.C.* History of Greece, vol. 5. London: W. B. Clive, University Tutorial Press, Ltd., [1894]. Few notes, a chronological and analytical table with dates in the left margin, test questions, a family tree, and a chapter on contemporary literature. According to Adolf Holm, the work is "pure vulgarisation."

8 Altheim, Franz. *Alexander und Asien; Geschichte eines Geistigen Erbs.* Tübingen: M. Niemeyer, 1953. Tr. into French by H. H. del Medico as *Alexandre et l'Asie, Histoire d'un Legs Spirituel.* Paris: Payot, 1954. Maps, and a bibliography after each chapter, but no footnotes. A volume of interest to all those interested in this period of history.

9 ———. *Zarathustra und Alexander; eine Ost-Westliche Begegnung.* Frankfurt am Main: Fischer Bücherie, 1960. A chronological table for 599/8 B.C. to 651 A.D., a map of Alexander's travels, a bibliography, and an index, but no notes. A discussion of the idealogical differences between the world of Alexander and that of the Near East. Especially valuable for the author's knowledge of German publications.

10 American Numismatic Society. *The Alexander Coinage of Sicyon.* Numismatic Studies No. 6. N. Y.: American Numismatic Society, 1950. Arranged from the notes of Edward T. Newell with

comments and notes added by Sydney P. Noe with a catalog of coins, footnotes, an index of symbols, and numerous plates.

11 Andreae, Bernard. *Das Alexandermosaik.* Opus Nobile, no. 14. Bremen: Walter Dorn Verlag, 1959. A short undocumented pamphlet with large illustrations and a bibliography of both ancient and modern sources.

12 Andreotti, Roberto. *Il Problema Politico di Alessandro Magno.* [Turin]: Società Editrice Internazionale, 1933. Many notes but no bibliography or index. A political history by the director of the Institute of Ancient History at the University of Parma, Italy.

13 Baege, Werner. "De Macedonum Sacris." Unpublished dissertation, Halle, 1913. Published in Halis: Formis Descripsit Ehrhard Karras, 1913; also, *Halle. Universität. Dissertationes Philologicae Halenses,* XXII (1913), 1-244. A table of contents, notes, a list of abbreviations, a vita of the author, and extensive quotations from classical sources for each deity discussed.

14 Ballester Escales, R[afael]. *Alejandro Magno.* Biografias, 4. 1st. ed. Barcelona: Ediciones Toray, 1963. No notes or bibliography, but it does have a detailed index. Part of a biographical series by an award-winning university lecturer.

15 Balogh, Elemér. *Political Refugees in Ancient Greece from the Period of the Tyrants to Alexander the Great.* Johannesburg: Witwatersrand University Press, 1943. A list of abbreviations, a name and subject index, a source index, and many notes. A valuable and stimulating, though short, study by a distinguished jurist.

16 Bamm, Peter. [Emmrich, Kurt]. *Alexander; oder, die Verwandlung der Welt.* Zurich: Droemer, [1965]. Trs. by J. Maxwell Brownjohn as *Alexander the Great; Power as Destiny.* N. Y.: McGraw, 1968. Includes a fold-out map and many illustrations, but unfortunately no index or bibliography. Some color illustrations were added to the English-language edition. An attempt to combine history, art and biography that does not succeed because it lacks a theme. Although a review in the *New Yorker* praises it, M. I. Finley describes it as ". . . a picture book for Christmas . . . an international coffee-table book."

17 Banerjee, Gauranga Nath. *Hellenism in Ancient India.* Calcutta:
    Butterworth, 1919. 2d. ed. by the same publisher in 1920. 3d. ed.
    rev. in Delhi: Munshi Ram Manohar Lal, 1961. Notes, a
    bibliography after each section with additional sources in the text.
    The author shows a remarkably wide range of reading and con-
    siderable critical ability. His judgment is eminently sensible.
    However, a review in the *Journal of Hellenic Studies* states that
    the last portion dealing with religion and philosophy" . . . is much
    too ambitious and lacks lucidity." The same review also notes
    that the volume could have been much shorter since many of the
    quotations from original sources were unnecessary as were some
    of the sources listed in the bibliographies.

18 Barbié du Bocage, [Victor Amédée]. *Analyse de la Carte des
    Marches et de l'Empire d'Alexandre-Le-Grand.* No imprint.
    Three fold-out maps, many notes, and additional sources are
    mentioned in the text. An analysis of some nineteenth-century
    maps by an eminent geographer.

19 Barker, Ernest, ed. and tr. *From Alexander to Constantine; Passages
    and Documents Illustrating the History of Social and Political
    Ideas, 336 B.C.-A.D. 337.* N. Y.: Oxford University Press, 1956;
    Oxford: Clarendon Press, 1956. A general index, an index of
    ancient authors whose works are here translated, a chronological
    table, and many footnotes. An anthology of translated passages
    with notes and comments concerning the whole history of Greek
    and Roman political ideas in ancient times. According to Victor
    Ehrenberg, its rich contents are readable, instructive, and interesting.
    It contains much to intrigue and interest both the classicist
    and the student of political history.

*20 Baruchello, Leopoldo. *Polisperconte e la Famiglia di Alessandro
    Magno.* Roma, 1892.

21 Bassfreund, Heinrich. "Alexander der Grosse und Josephus."
    Unpublished dissertation, Universität zu Giessen, 1920.
    No bibliography, but the notes are collected at the end.

22 Baumbach, Alfred. "Kleinasien unter Alexander dem Grossen."
    Unpublished dissertation, Universität Jena, 1911. Published
    Weida i. Th.: Druck von Thomas and Hubert, 1911. Many notes,

an index, a chronology of events for 334-331, tables of satraps
according to various authors, and a vita of the author.

23 Bell, H. Idris. *Egypt from Alexander the Great to the Arab
   Conquest*; *A Study in the Diffusion and Decay of Hellenism*.
   Oxford: Clarendon Press, 1948 and 1956. Many notes, a bibliography, and an index. The Gregynog Lectures for 1946, revised
   and expanded for the non-specialist. The volume is notable
   for its accuracy and exacting standards of scholarship.

*24 *Bellezze della Storia Antica o Fatti e detti Memorabili dei Grand'
   Uomini che Sono Resi Illustri nella Politica, nelle Armi
   nell'Amministrazione degi Stati, dal Regno di Semiramide, Fino alla
   Divisione di Quello di Alessandro il Grande*. Verona, 1817.
   This anonymous work is mentioned in Berzuna's *A Tentative
   Classification* . . . .

25 Bellinger, Alfred Raymond. *Essays on the Coinage of Alexander
   the Great*. Numismatic Studies, No. 11. N. Y.: American
   Numismatic Society, 1963. Many notes, maps and illustrations;
   a bibliography and a chronological summary. The bibliography is
   particularly valuable because it assembles the widely scattered
   literature of the Alexander coinages. A probing discussion of the
   coinages in their historical and economic contexts.

26 Benoist-Mechin, Jacques Gabriel. *Alexandre le Grand*; *ou, Le Rêve
   Dépassé*. Lausanne: Clairefontaine, 1964. Tr. from the French by
   Mary Ilford as *Alexander the Great, the Meeting of East and
   West*. 1st. English Language edition. N. Y.: Hawthorn Books,
   1966. Illustrations, an index, a fold-out map, and a table of
   dynasties. The English edition puts the maps on the endpapers and
   omits the table of dynasties. A beautifully-produced volume that
   merely re-states already well-known facts.

*27 Bergenroth,   . "De Regia Potestate, qua Philippus II et
   Alexander M. apud Macedones usi sunt," a dissertation in
   *Nachricht von dem Gymnasium zu Thorn von Michaelis 1853
   bis Michaelis 1854* (Thorn, 1854).

28 Berger, Guilielmus. "De Q. Curti Rufi Aetate." Unpublished
    dissertation, Heidelberg, 1860. Later published at Carolsruhae:
    Excuderunt Malsche et Vogel, 1860. A brief, documented disserta-
    tion giving quotations in Greek from ancient sources.

29 Bernoulli, Johann-J[akob]. *Die Erhaltenen Darstellungen
    Alexanders des Grossen; ein Nachtrag zur Griechischen Ikonogra-
    phie.* Munich: F. Bruckmann, 1905. Many plates, an index,
    many footnotes, but no formal bibliography (works cited in text).
    A popular presentation which contains little that is new for the
    scholar. Friedrich Hauser comments that what is new could have
    been stated in a short periodical article.

30 Bertolotti, Mario. *La Critica Medica Nella Storia Alessandro Magno.*
    Torino: Bocca Fratelli, [1932]. A table of contents, illustrations,
    notes, a list of clinical terms, and a bibliography in the notes
    collected at the end. A medical discussion about Alexander
    by an Italian radiologist.

31 Berve, Helmut. *Das Alexanderreich auf Prosographischer Grundlage.*
    2 vols. in 1. Munich: C. H. Beck, 1926. An index (to vol. 1
    only), a bibliography which is extensive in German dissertations,
    and a family tree. The first volume is a fairly complete summary
    of evidence in ancient records about Alexander's life and the
    organization of his army and empire. The second volume is a
    dictionary listing of known facts concerning everyone whose
    name occurs in any connection with Alexander (833 entries).

*32 Berzuna, Julius. "A Comparison of the Life of Alexander the
    Great with an Old Spanish Poem of the XIIIth. Century."
    Unpublished dissertation, University of Illinois, 1923. Unavailable
    in the U. S.—copy at the University of Illinois is now "lost."

33 ————. *A Tentative Classification of Books, Pamphlets and
    Pictures Concerning Alexander the Great and the Alexander
    Romances, from the Collection of Julio Berzuna.* [Durham?,
    N. H.]: Private Printing, 1939. Plates, a partial index,
    and lists of various editions.

34 Beurlier, Aemilius. *De Divinis Honoribus Quos Acceperunt
    Alexander et Successores Ejus.* Paris: Ernestum Thorin, 1890.
    Also a dissertation, Faculté des Lettres de Paris, 1890. Many foot-

notes, a chronology of the Ptolemys, but no bibliography. An
excellent study in the cults of the Greek kings. The author is well
informed and knows the current literature. Georges Radet termed
the volume a clear and solid contribution on a large and very
interesting problem.

35 Bevan, Edwyn. *The House of Ptolemy. A History of Egypt under
the Ptolemaic Dynasty.* Vol. 4 of *The History of Egypt.* Edited by
Sir Flinders Petrie. London: E. Arnold, 1902. London: Methuen,
1927. Reprinted in Chicago: Argonaut, 1968. A table of
contents, many notes, illustrations with an index for them, a list
of abbreviations, and an index. This volume was designed to
replace the volume by the same title written in 1899 and revised
in 1914 by J. P. Mahaffy. A chronological narrative of the political
history of Egypt under the 14 Ptolemies. The volume is of value
for its full citations in English of original documents and for
the critical judgment of the author. A book for every student
of the Hellenistic world.

36 Bevan, Wilson Lloyd. *World's Leading Conquerors. Alexander
the Great, Caesar, Charles the Great, the Ottoman Sultans, the
Spanish Conquisadors, Napoleon.* N. Y.: Henry Holt and Co.,
1913. A table of contents, portraits, and an index. One in a
series of biographies designed to give the general reader
substantial and detailed information.

37 Bieber, Margarete. *Alexander the Great in Greek and Roman Art.*
Chicago: Argonaut, 1964. A general index and many plates.
It is essentially a reprint of an earlier useful study of portraits of
Alexander published in the Proceedings of the American
Philosophical Society (1949) with insertions made for newly
identified portraits. The texts remains virtually unchanged,
although the bibliography has been revised. According to R. V.
Nicholls, "This extremely readable book is the most important
contribution on the subject that we have . . . ."

38 ———. *The Sculpture of the Hellenistic Age.* N. Y.: Columbia
University Press, 1955. Rev. ed. by the same publisher in 1961.
A chronology, a select bibliography, an index, and many plates.
An admirably up-to-date handbook and guide by a classical scholar;
an invaluable storehouse of information for students, teachers,

and librarians. A substantial and finely produced book that will long remain a standard source of information.

39 Birt, Theodore. *Alexander der Grosse und das Weltgriechentum bis zum Erscheinen Jesu.* Leipzig: Quelle and Meyer, [1925]. Many plates and line drawings with the notes collected at the end. Printed in the old German script. The volume was not written for the specialist but for the young student with some interest in antiquity. The author's familiarity with the classical literature and with the spiritual life of the period is especially helpful.

*40 Bonfanti, Giovanni. *Vita d'Alessandro Magno Scritta.* n.d. ca. 1820. The title is listed in Berzuna's *Tentative Classification* . . . .

41 Boucher, Arthur. *L'Art de Vaincre aux Deux Pôles de l'Histoire: Sa Loi Eternelle. Homère, Sparte et Athènes, Alexandre, Napoléon, la Grande Guerre.* Nancy and Paris: Berger-Levrault, 1928. An expanded table of contents, diagrams, maps, tables, but no notes, index, or bibliography. A study of the conception of war in antiquity by a scholar and distinguished Hellenist.

*42 Bovis, René de. *Alexandre le Grand sur le Danube.* Reims, 1908.

43 Brandis, Johannes. *Das Münz-, Mass- und Gewichtswesen in Vorderaisen bis auf Alexander den Grossen.* Berlin: Verlag von Wilhelm Hertz, 1866. A bibliography, an index, various tables, and a catalog of coins by mint with descriptions and locations. A volume concerning the Alexander coinage of the Asian frontier by a noted archaeologist, philosopher, and decipherer of inscriptions.

44 Breccia, E. *Municipalite d'Alexandrie. Alexandrea ad Aegyptum; Guide de la Ville Ancienne et Moderne et du Musee Greco-Romain.* Bergamo: Istuto Italiano d'Arti Grafiche, 1914. *Alexandria Municipality. Alexandrea ad Aegyptum; a Guide to the Ancient and Modern Town and to Its Graeco-Roman Museum.* By the same publisher in 1922. Many photographs (some in color), maps, and a excellent bibliography after each section. A guide to Alexandria, both ancient and modern. The 1922 edition was considerably enlarged and revised. It gives a concise description of the city with summaries of its history and the topography of the ancient city and of excavated remains.

45 Breebart, Abraham Benjamin. *Enige Historiografische Aspecten van Arrianus' Anabasis Alexandri.* Leidse Historische Reeks van de Rijksuniversiteit te Leiden, Deel IV. Leiden: Universitaire Pers, 1960. Many footnotes, a good bibliography, and a summary in English. A study in the method and way of thinking of Arrian. According to Stewart I. Oost, the volume contains some startling ideas and unsuccessful arguments. He concludes that, "This is not an important book, but it is a useful one to read."

46 Breloer, Bernhard. *Alexanders Bund Mit Poros. Indien von Dareios zu Sandrokottos.* Sammlung Orientalistischen Arbeiten, 9. Leipzig: Harrassowitz, 1941. Expanded table of contents, notes, diagrams of the battle, and a list of abbreviations. A valuable study.

47 ———. *Alexanders Kampf gegen Poros; ein Beitrag zur Indischen Geschichte.* Bonner Orientalistische Studien, Heft 3. Stuttgart: Verlag W. Kohlhammer, 1933. Plates, a large map, footnotes, and a bibliography. A discussion of the topography and sources used by Arrian and Ptolemy for the battle. The volume is valuable for its description of topography, but the reconstruction of the battle does not follow the Greek texts. W. W. Tarn's review states that ". . . Breloer's battle was not Alexander's."

48 Bretzel, Hugo. *Botanische Forschungen des Alexanderzuges.* Leipzig: B. G. Teubner, 1903. Part of this work appeared as his dissertation at the Universität Strassburg in 1902 under the title: "Botanische Forschungen des Alexanderzuges nach Griechischen General-stabsberichten." Maps, an index, many diagrams of plants, and an exact listing of growth forms as recorded by Theophrastus.

49 Brown, Truesdell Sparhawk. *Onesicritus: A Study in Hellenistic Historiography.* Berkeley and Los Angeles: University of California Press, 1949. Many notes, a bibliography, an index of Greek terms, and a general index. According to G. T. Griffith, it is a well-written and impartial inspection of the evidence concerning the role of the man who piloted Alexander's ship down the Indus. Originally issued as a dissertation at Columbia University in the same year.

50 Browne, Laurence E. *Ezekiel and Alexander*. London: S.P.C.K.,
    1952. A table of "Ezekiel's Dated Prophecies" and notes.
    The author is a student of Islam and has been a professor of
    comparative religion and of theology.

51 Brunner, Franz. "Die Politischen Flüchtlinge in Griechenland in
    der Zeit von der Tyrannis bis zum Rückberufungsdekret Alexanders
    des Grossen." Unpublished dissertation, Universität Wien, 1962.
    A table of contents, notes, a bibliography, chronological tables
    for types of government in different areas, an alphabetical list by
    place of governments, many quotations from ancient sources,
    and a vita of the author.

52 Burgard, Raymond. *L'Expédition d'Alexandre et la Conquête
    de l'Asie*. [Paris]: Gallimard, [1937]. Maps, diagrams, and
    plates, few notes, a brief résumé before each chapter, a list of
    principle works consulted, but no index. A popular presentation
    which concentrates on the campaigns of Alexander. The
    bibliography is very short and imprecise, and the volume lacks
    useful notes.

53 Burn, Andrew Robert. *Alexander the Great and the Hellenistic
    Empire*. London: Hodder and Stoughton for the English Uni-
    versities Press, 1947. N. Y.: Macmillan, 1948. London: English
    Universities Press, [1956]. New enl. ed. N. Y.: Collier Books,
    1962. 2d. ed. London: English Universities Press, 1964. A short,
    annotated bibliography and a good index, but no footnotes.
    A scholarly chronological history written with brilliance and
    charm, which also points out Alexander's relation to the period
    following his death.

54 Buschor, Ernst. *Maussollos und Alexander*. Munich: C. H. Beck,
    [1950]. Many notes and 65 plates, but there is no index or
    bibliography. The attempt to reassign surviving pieces of sculpture
    of the Mausoleum has been criticized severely.

55 Capelle, W. *Alexanders Siegeszug durch Asien*. Zurich, 1950.

56 Cary, Max. *A History of the Greek World from 323 to 146 B. C.*
    N. Y.: Macmillan, 1939. 2d. ed. by the same publisher in 1951.
    New ed. in N. Y.: Barnes and Noble, 1963. Three maps, a valuable
    select bibliography (revised for the 1963 ed.), a complete index,

and "Lists and Stemmata of the Hellenistic Dynasties." The second
edition is a reprint of the first with changes that could be made
without resetting. P. M. Fraser criticized the second edition for
the old bibliography that had been retained. However, this
was corrected in the third edition. A careful and thoughtful
treatment with sustained readability. Its scholarship and clarity
make good reading for the general reader.

57 ———. *The Legacy of Alexander; A History of the Greek World
from 323 to 146 B.C.* N. Y.: Dial Press, 1932. Published in
Gt. Britain as *A History of the Greek World from 323 to 146 B.C.*
London: Methuen, [1932]. An index, 3 maps, and a select
bibliography. A scholarly history with a wealth of information.
It is the third volume in Methuen's History of the Greek and
Roman World.

58 Cholpanov, Boris. *Aleksandŭr Makedonski.* Sofia: World Military
Publishing House, 1964. Diagrams, a map, and many footnotes,
but no references to other sources. Written in Bulgarian.

59 Chys, Peter Otto van der. "Specimen Academicum Inaugurale
Exhibens Commentarium Geotraphicum in Arrianum de
Expeditione Alexandri." Unpublished dissertation, Academia
Lugduno Batava, 1828. Published in Lugduni Batavorum:
J. C. Cyfveer, 1828. Index, fold-out map, quotations in Greek from
ancient sources, few notes, and sources in the text. A useful work
even today, although much out-dated. The weakest portion,
according to Droysen, is that section which deals with the
campaigns of 329-328 B. C.

*60 Cipolla, Arnaldo. *Sulle Orme di Alessandro Magno, dal Granico
al Cispio.* Verona, 1933. The Cleveland Public Library's copy
is not available for loan.

61 Clarke, Edward Daniel. *The Tomb of Alexander; a Dissertation
on the Sarcophagus Brought from Alexandria and Now in the
British Museum.* Cambridge: Printed by R. Watts at the
University Press, 1805. Many footnotes, some marginal notes,
and illustrations. A volume showing enterprise and research by a
well-known traveller, antiquarian, mineralogist, and scholar.

62 Cloché, Paul. *Alexandre le Grand et les Essais de Fusion entre l'Occident Greco-Macedonien et l'Orient*. Neuchâtel: H. Messeiller, [1953]. Que Sais-Je, No. 622. Paris: Presses Universitaires, 1954. Does not include footnotes, bibliography, or index, simply a table of contents. A. H. M. Jones criticizes the author for his inclusion of needlessly long and detailed accounts of the eastern campaigns. Furthermore, Jones notes that an undocumented account is ". . . hardly a suitable place to set forth individual and controversial views." Therefore, he warns that the volume is ". . . not to be recommended to any but experts who can test its statements."

63 ————. *Histoire de la Macédoine Jusqu'à l'Avenèment d'Alexandre le Grand (336 avant J.-C.)*. Paris: Payot, 1960. A map of Greece—regrettably not one of Macedonia—few notes, and a bibliography following each chapter. An original and profound contribution by one of the foremost Hellenists of this period. A useful work, especially because of its use of ancient texts, epigraphy, and archaeology.

64 Cohen, Robert. *La Grèce et l'Hellenisation du Monde Antique*. Paris: Presses Universitaires de France, 1934. New ed. by the same publisher in 1948. A long and thorough bibliographic essay and bibliographic notes at the end of each chapter except the first. A survey of the whole field of ancient Greek history, primarily intended for advanced French students. It contains a concise and valuable résumé of the state of the questions treated at the time of publication.

65 Colocotronis, V. *La Macédoine et l'Hellenisme. Étude Historique et Ethnologique*. Paris: Berger-Levrault, 1919. A table of contents, illustrations, tables, fold-out maps, a list of plates, and an extensive bibliography; it is a useful, scholarly volume.

66 Crämer, Hermann. "Beiträge zur Geschichte Alexanders des Grossen." Unpublished dissertation, Marburg, 1893. Many notes, an index, and a vita for the author.

67 Cummings, Lewis Vance. *Alexander the Great*. Boston: Houghton Mifflin, 1940. Many maps, an index, and a few footnotes. A well organized, well-documented, extremely conscientious and accurate book which is also most readable.

68 Cunningham, Alexander. *The Ancient Geography of India Including the Campaigns of Alexander*. London: Trübner and Co., 1871. Later published as *Cunningham's Ancient Geography of India*. Ed. with an introd. and notes by Surendranath Majumar Sastri. Calcutta: Chuckervertty, Chatterjee and Co., 1924. Published under the original title in Varanasi: Indological Book House, 1963. Many notes, maps, and an index. An elaborate work of great learning for which the author personally travelled over the entire country to fix the line of Alexander's campaigns.

69 Curteis, Arthur Mapletoff. . . . *Rise of the Macedonian Empire*. Epochs of Ancient History. London: Longmans, Green and Co., 1877. Later editions by the same publisher in 1881 and 1882. N. Y.: Scribner's Sons, 1887. Eight maps, subject guides in the margins, a chronological table, and an index, but no notes. Designed for the general public. Now very much out-of-date and of little value.

70 Cutrules, Alexander James. *Invictus*; *A History of Alexander the Great*. 1st. ed. N. Y.: Vantage Press, 1958. A chronology for 356-323 B.C. and a brief bibliography, but no footnotes or index. A popularized biography for the general adult reader.

*71 Dahmen, J. *Auswahl aus der Geschichte Alexanders des Grossen*. Münster: Ascherdorff, 1914. The title is reviewed in *Blatter für das Bayerische Gymnasial-Schulwesen* for 1914.

72 Dascalakis, Apostolos Basileiou. *The Hellenism of the Ancient Macedonians*. Athens: [University of Athens], 1960. English ed. Thessaloniki: Institute for Balkan Studies, 1965. Many notes, a map, an index, and a bibliography. Most chapters were previously published as articles in learned journals generally inaccessible to Americans. An impressive, scholarly work that is lavishly documented. A definitive study of the problem of the Hellenism of Macedonians. The author shows a formidable command of all the original sources and of modern literature.

73 ————. *'O Megas 'Alexandros kaì 'o 'Ellēnismós*. Athens: Historical Seminar of the University, 1963. Tr. into English by the Institute for Balkan Studies as: *Alexander the Great and Hellenism*. Thessaloniki: Institute for Balkan Studies, 1966. A bibliography, references at the end of each part, and an index of names.

A series of nine studies designed to illustrate Alexander and the most important aspects of his career as the exponent of Greek civilization. A handsomely produced book whose translation is inadequate. The original was in a highly patriotic style, and it was designed to appeal more to the author's contemporaries in Greece than to scholars of ancient history.

74 Diem, Carl. *Alexander der Grosse als Sportsmann.* Frankfurt am Main: Wilhelm Impert, [1957]. A 32 pp. pamphlet containing a portrait, a bibliography, but no footnotes (sources mentioned in the text). The author is a professor and director of physical education at the University of Cologne and has been the sports consultant to the German Federal Government and Secretary to the General German Committee for Physical Education.

75 Diller, Aubrey. *Race Mixture Among the Greeks Before Alexander.* Illinois Studies in Language and Literature, vol. 20, pt. 1. Urbana: University of Illinois Press, 1937. Many notes, a bibliography, an index to sources, and an index to Greek words. A partial study of race mixture in Athens down to 322 B.C. Because it was not intended to be a complete study, it is uneven, lacks unity, and contains much that is dubious and needs further study. Originally issued as "Studies of Race Mixture Among the Greeks Before Alexander," a dissertation at the University of Illinois in 1930.

*76 Dimitsa, U. G. *'Alexandrivòs Dia Ēosmos.* Athens, 1889.

*77 ———. *'Istoria tēs 'Archaias Póleōs 'Alexandreias.* Athens, 1885.

78 Dittberner, Walter Otto Karl. "Issos. Ein Beitrag zur Geschichte Alexanders des Grossen." Unpublished dissertation, Friedrich-Wilhelms Universität zu Berlin, 1907. Also published in Berlin: Verlag Georg Nauck (Fritz Rühe), 1907. Many notes, diagrams, a map, but no index or bibliography.

79 Dodge, Theodore Ayrault. *Great Captains. Alexander; A History of the Origin and Growth of the Art of War from the Earliest Times to the Battle of Ipsus, B.C. 301, with a Detailed Account of the Campaigns of the Great Macedonian.* N.Y.: Houghton, Mifflin and Co., 1890. Maps, a genealogy of Alexander, an index, but no

footnotes or bibliography. A just summary of Alexander, occupying itself mainly with military marches.

80 ———. *Great Captains: A Course of Six Lectures Showing the Influence on the Art of War of the Campaigns of Alexander, Hannibal, Caesar, Gustavus Adolphus, Frederick, and Napoleon.* N. Y.: Houghton, Mifflin, 1889. A series of lectures delivered in Boston under the auspices of the Lowell Institute in January, 1889. Contains maps and diagrams, but no footnotes or bibliography. Critical, just and sensible studies of the personalities of these great men.

81 Dosson, S. "Étude sur Quinte Curce, Sa Vie et Son Oeuvre." Unpublished dissertation, Faculté des Lettres de Paris, 1886. Published in Paris: Librairie Hachette, 1886. An expanded table of contents, notes, a listing of sources in each section, comparisons of texts of various classical authors, and appendices dealing with manuscripts of Curtius. Provocative research on the problems of of the biography of Quintus Curtius.

82 Droysen, Hans. *Untersuchungen Über Alexander des Grossen Heerwesen und Kriegführung.* Freiburg I. B.: Akademische Verlagsbuchhandlung von J. C. B. Mohr (Paul Siebeck), 1885. Many footnotes and a table for the number of soldiers, but no index or bibliography. A new edition of the manual by Hermann. An interesting study on the composition and organization of Alexander's army.

83 Droysen, Johann Gustav. *Geschichte Alexanders des Grossen.* Berlin: G. Fenke, 1833. Berlin: R. V. Decker, 1917. New ed. Leipzig: Alfred Kröner, 1931. Dusseldorf: Droste, c1966. A chronology of events but no footnotes, index, or bibliography. A work by the accredited historiographer of Prussia. According to A. W. Ward, the volume is an ". . . historical work of high interest and marked originality of treatment, being designed to vindicate the unification of Greece as well as the Hellenisation of Asia."

84 ———. *Geschichte des Hellenismus.* 6 vol. in 3. Gotha: F. A. Perthes, 1877-78. Paris: Ernest Leroux, 1883-85 (French ed.). New ed. Basel: Benno Schwabe, c1951-53. Many notes, an index, and maps. The French edition includes a chronological list of Macedonian kings from 337 to 220 B.C., and a bibliography for

the set. According to Ulrich Wilcken, the extraordinary scholarship of the set marks the beginning of modern Alexander scholarship.

85 ———. *Kleine Schriften zur Alten Geschichte*. 2 vols. Leipzig: Verlag von Veit and Co., 1893-94. A collection of essays with a table of contents, notes in some articles, a list of Droysen's works, his portrait and signature. An excellent collection of essays on various aspects of ancient history.

86 Durant, Will[iam James]. *The Story of Civilization*. vol. II. *The Life of Greece, being a History of Greek Civilization from the Beginnings, and of Civilization in the Near East from the Death of Alexander, to the Roman Conquest; with an Introduction on the Prehistoric Culture of Crete*: N. Y.: Simon and Schuster, 1939. A chronological table at the beginning of each period, maps, a glossary of foreign words, a bibliography, many notes, and a pronouncing and biographical index. A popularized presentation that is well balanced and well documented. The author's sound judgments and concise style make the book both highly readable and stimulating.

87 Dzięcol, Witold. *Aleksander Wielki Macedoński*. London: "Veritas" Foundation Press, 1963. Diagrams, notes by chapter, index, fold-out map, and a "Summary: Alexander the Great of Macedon" in English.

88 Ebeling, Erich. *Geschichte des Orients vom Tode Alexanders des Grossen bis zum Einbruch des Islams*. Berlin: de Gruyter, 1939. A table of contents, a chronology for 323 B.C. to 651 A.D., a fold-out map, a bibliography, and an index, but no notes. A brief essay printed in the old German type. A concise survey for the general public. However, H. Bengtson noted that the chronology should not be taken literally because of several errors.

89 Eddy, Samuel K. *The King Is Dead; Studies in the Near East Resistance to Hellenism, 334-31 B.C.* Lincoln: University of Nebraska Press, 1961. Many footnotes, a full bibliography, index, and a fold-out map. A systematic discussion of the legacy of Alexander in the Near East, region by region, class by class. An excellent book.

90 Ehrenberg, Victor. *Alexander and the Greeks*. Trans. by Ruth
   Fraenkel von Velsen. Oxford: Basil Blackwell, 1938. An attractively
   printed collection of 4 essays with notes which carefully reviews
   all evidence concerning Alexander's relation to the "liberated"
   cities of Greece. An interesting book though far from easy to read
   because of the imperfect translation. A review by C. A. Robinson, Jr.
   states that it ". . . abounds in correct and stimulating suggestions,
   and in guesses which may be right . . . ."

91 ———. *Alexander und Ägypten*. Beiheft zum "Alten Orient,"
   Heft 7. Leipzig: J. C. Hinrichs, 1926. Many notes but no index
   or bibliography. An analysis of the motives and principles which
   underlay the policy of Alexander in regard to Egypt and to his
   theory of empire. An interesting piece of work by an eminent
   scholar—well worth reading.

92 ———. "Die Opfer Alexanders an der Indusmündung," in
   Festschrift Moriz Winternitz. Leipzig: Otto Harrassowitz, 1933,
   287-97. Many footnotes.

93 Eicke, Ludovicus. "Veterum Philosophorum Qualia Fuerint de
   Alexandro Magno Iudica." Unpublished dissertation, Rostock,
   1909. Many notes, an index, and a vita of the author, but no
   bibliography.

94 Endres, Heinrich. *Geographischer Horizont und Politik bei
   Alexander den Grossen*. Würzburg: J. C. Becker, 1924. A well-
   footnoted 23 pp. pamphlet containing neither index nor bibliography, by a librarian and professor at the University of Würzburg.

95 ———. "Die Offiziellen Grundlagen der Alexanderüberlieferung
   und das Werk des Ptolemäus; Quellenkritische Studien zur
   Alexandergeschichte." Unpublished dissertation, Würzburg, 1913.
   A table of contents but no bibliography or index, and a vita
   of the author. Printed in the old German type.

96 Fabietti, Ettore. *La Conquista di Alessandro*. Milan: Antonio
   Vallardi, [1940]. Table of contents, illustrations, some notes,
   and maps.

*97 Falk. *Ueber den Geschichtl. Werth von Plut. Lebensbeschr.
   Alex. d. Gr.* Lauban, 1833. The title is listed in Kluge's
   De Itinerario Alexandri Magni (1861).

98 Ferguson, William Scott. *Hellenistic Athens; an Historical Essay.*
London: Macmillan, 1911. Many footnotes, a bibliography,
and an index. A reconstruction of municipal life from the death
of Alexander (323 B.C.) to the sack of the city by Sulla in 86 B.C.
Not an easy book to read due to its mass of detail, but it is able
and learned.

99 Fontana, Maria José. *Le Lotte per la Successione di Alessandro
Magno dal 323 al 315.* Palermo: [Presso l'Accademia], 1960.
Many notes but no index or bibliography. A study in the aims and
motives of the principal leaders of the Empire after Alexander's
death. The author handles complex issues skillfully and judiciouly.
The appendices give a full and valuable study of literary sources.
Reprinted from the *Atti dell'Accademia di Scienze Lettere e Arti
di Palermo,* ser. IV, XVIII (1957-58), pt. 2.

100 Fränkel, Arthur. *Die Quellen der Alexanderhistoriker; ein Beitrag
zur Griechischen.* Breslau: J. U. Kern (Max Müller), 1883.
A detailed table of contents, some footnotes, but no index or
bibliography. An elaborate work with good comparisons of
Plutarch, Arrian, Curtius, and Diodorus.

101 Fuhrmann, Heinrich. *Philoxenos von Eretria. Archäologische
Untersuchungen über Zwei Alexandermosaike.* Göttingen:
W. Fr. Kaestner, 1931. An expanded table of contents, a long list
of abbreviations, illustrations, family tree, tables, diagram to
show locations of mosaics, and notes which are collected at the end.

102 Fuller, John Frederick Charles. *The Generalship of Alexander
the Great.* London: Eyre and Spottiswoode, 1958. New Brunswick,
N. J.: Rutgers University Press, 1960. A map of Alexander's
route on the endpapers, many illustrations, battle plans, many
footnotes, and an index. An historical reconstruction of Alexander's
campaigns, strategy, and tactics written by a professional
military man.

103 De Geer, Bartholdus Jacobus Lintelo. "Specimen Historicum
de Eumene Cardiano A. Caeteris Alexandri Magni Ducibus Rite
Distinguendo, Quod, Supremo Favente Numine ex Auctoritate
Rectoris Magnifici Richardi van Rees." Unpublished dissertation,
Academin Rheno-Trajectina, 1838. Published in *Trajecti ad
Rhenum: Apud Kemink et Filium,* 1838. A table of contents,

notes, quotations in Greek from ancient sources, a chronological table from 361-316 B.C., and a list of "Quaestiones."

104 Geier, Robert. *Alexander und Aristoteles in Ihren Gegenseitigen Beziehungen.* Halle: Verlag der Buchhandlung des Waisen hauses, 1856. A well-documented volume printed in the old German type.

105 ————. *Alexandri M. Historiarum Scriptores Aetate Suppares.* Leipzig: Sumptibus Librarie Gebaueriae, 1844. Many footnotes, an index, an index of contemporary authors and remaining fragments—containing a list of fragments with text for each author, and comments. The author breaks with his predecessors in concluding that Arrian used many more sources than had previously been believed—i.e., Ptolemy, Aristobulus, and Nearchus.

106 Geier, Samuelis Robertus. "Commentationis de Alexandri M. Rerum Scriptoribus Particula." Unpublished dissertation, Halle, 1835. Published in Halle: Typis Expressum Ploetzianis, 1835. Notes, "Sententiae Controversae," and a vita of the author.

*107 Geiger, N. *Alexanders Feldzuge in Sogdiana.* Progr. d. Neustadt, 1884. The title is listed in Pohlmann's *Griechische Geschichte und Quellenkunde.*

*108 Genssler, G. *Die Schlacht bei Gaugamela.* Programm Pruem, 1873.

109 Geschwandtner, Leo. "Quibus Fontibus Trogus Pompeius in Rebus Successorum Alexandri M. Enarrandis Usus Sit." Unpublished dissertation, Academia Fridericiana Halens, 1878. A vita of the author; "sententiae controversae"; notes; and a comparison of the texts of Justin and Diodorus, Justin and Plutarch, and Plutarch and Arrian.

110 Geyer, Fritz. *Alexander der Grosse und die Diadochen.* Wissenschaft und Bildung; Einzeldarstellungen aus allen Gebieten des Wissens, 213. Leipzig: Quelle und Meyer, 1925. Table of contents, index, annotated bibliography, but no notes. Printed in the old German type.

111 Gitti, Alberto. *Alessandro Magno All'Oasi di Siwah; Il Problema delle Fonti*. Bari: Adriatica Editrice, [1951]. Many notes, a good bibliography with references to more than 100 books and periodicals, and an index. A systematic discussion of the problems of the origins and transmissions of ancient sources. One value of the volume stems from the reasoning and scholarship upon which its conclusions are based. A. R. Burn judges it particularly useful to scholars making a first examination of the scattered literature about Alexander.

112 Glotz, Gustav. *Histoire Generale. Histoire Ancienne, Deuxieme Partie, Histoire Grecque*, Vol. IV, "Alexandre et l'Hellenisation du Monde Antique." Paris: Presses Universitaires de France, 1938. 2d. ed. by same publisher, 1945. Many notes, an index, maps, an expanded table of contents, and a full bibliography on the first page of each chapter. A standard work displaying up-to-date scholarship and sound judgment. W. W. Tarn comments that the sections by Roussel are perfectly competent; those by Cohen are written with judgment and moderation to give a good idea of the man and his story.

113 Glück, Maximilianus. "De Tyro ab Alexandro Magno Oppugnata et Capta. Quaestiones de Fontibus ad Alexandri Magni Historiam Pertinentibus." Unpublished dissertation, Universitate Albertina Regimontana, 1886. Published in Regimontana; Ex Officina Liedtkiana, 1886. Notes, comparisons of texts of Curtius and Arrian and of Curtius and Diodorus, and a vita of the author. The conclusions drawn by the author are somewhat questionable.

114 Gobdelas, Démétrius P. de. [François de Salignac de la Mothe Fénelon]. *Histoire d'Alexandre le Grand Suivant les Écrivains Orientaux*. Varsovie: l'Imprimerie de N. Glücksberg, Imprimeur-Libraire de l'Université, 1822. A great number of notes (pp. 86-202), a list of subscribers, but no table of contents, index, or bibliography. Extracts from lectures by a famous French prelate and professor of mathematics.

115 Granier, Friedrich. *Die Makedonische Heeresversammlung; Eine Beitrag zum Antiken Staatsrecht*. Münchener Beiträge zur Papyrusforschung, 13. Munich: C. H. Beck, 1931. Expanded table of contents, notes, index, and a good bibliography. Development

of a dissertation done at the University of Berlin in 1921.
According to W. W. Tarn it displays a lack of knowledge of
work done outside Germany but is valuable as a full collection
of materials and sources on the subject of the Macedonian army.

116 Gregor, Joseph. *Alexander der Grosse; Die Weltherrschaft einer
Idee*. München: R. Piper, [1940]. An expanded table of contents,
illustrations, a list of illustrations, a fold-out map, and an index,
but no notes. A broad political and cultural history of the Greek
world in the fourth century with a review of Alexander's
personality.

*117 Grenz, Siegfried. "Beiträge zur Geschichte des Diadems in den
Hellenistischen Reichen." Unpublished dissertation, Universität
Greifswald, 1914. An abstract was later published in Breslau:
Druck der Breslauer Genoffenschafts-Buchdruckerei, 1921.
The abstract is available in the United States from the Center for
Research Libraries.

118 Griffith, Guy Thompson, ed. *Alexander the Great; the Main
Problems*. N. Y.: Barnes and Noble, 1966. Many footnotes, an
appended bibliography, but no index. This is the third volume in a
useful series of photographic reprints of groups of papers. A
series of 16 papers derived from 10 periodicals, 2 of which are
rare in Britain. A. R. Burn points out that an index would be a
welcome addition.

119 ————. *The Mercenaries of the Hellenistic World*. Cambridge:
University Press, 1935. A brief selective bibliography, many
footnotes, an index of technical terms, and a general index. There
is also a "list of all known mercenaries added" to Alexander's
army by place with classical sources cited. It is a valuable contribution to the study of the constitution of the armies of the
Macedonian kingdoms.

120 Grimmig, Friedrich. "Arrians Diadochengeschichte." Dissertation,
Königlichen Vereinigten Friedrichs-Universität, 1914. Published
in Halle (Saale): Druck von Ehrhardt Karras, 1914. Many notes,
long Greek quotations, a table of contents, a bibliography, a list
of satraps by country according to various ancient sources, and
a vita of the author.

*121 Grossi, A. *Alessandro Magno e i Romani*. Aquila, 1921.

122 Grote, Karl. "Das Griechische Soldnerwesen der Hellenistischen Zeit." Unpublished dissertation, Jena, 1913. Published in Weida i. Th.: Druck von Thomas & Hubert, 1913. An index and a short bibliography in the foreword.

123 Gruhn, Albert. *Das Schlachtfeld von Issus. Eine Widerlegung der Ansicht Jankes*. Jena: Hermann Costenoble, 1905. A fold-out map but no notes or bibliography. An attempt to establish the location of the battlefield of Issus. Edmund Lammert's review notes that whereas Gruhn's arguments are persuasive, they are not decisive. Subsequently Gruhn defended his thesis and produced additional arguments—BPW XXVI (1906), no. 8.

124 Guidobaldi, Domenico de. *Alessandro e Bucefalo Bassorilievo Pompeiano Scovato nel 1849*. Naples: Tipografia di Borel e Bompald, 1851. A table of contents, many notes, and some fold-out illustrations.

*125 Gutschmid, Alfred von. *Forschungen zur Geschichte Alexanders des Grossen*. Stuttgart, 1887.

126 ———. *Geschichte Irans und Seiner Nachbarländer von Alexander dem Grossen bis zum Untergang der Arsaciden*. Tübingen: H. Laupp'schen Buchhandlung, 1888. Originally written for the ninth edition of the *Encyclopaedia Britannica* where its English translation, considerably abridged, appears. No bibliography, no index, but many notes.

*127 Haaren, John Henry. *Famous Men of Greece*. Boston: University Publishing Co., [1904]. Unavailable for examination—only copy located in the United States at the Boston Public Library where it is noncirculating.

128 Habicht, Christian. *Gottmenschentum und Greichische Städte*. Zetemata. Monographien zur Klassischen Altertumswissenschaft, Heft 14. Munich: C. H. Beck, 1956. An expanded table of contents, a list of abbreviations, indexes (general, author, and inscription), notes, and a bibliography. A fundamental work based on his thesis written at Hamburg in 1951. Extremely useful for its monumental collection of parallel passages, its able arguments, and its sane

and balanced account of the worship of Greek rulers to the
middle of the third century B.C.

129 Hackmann, Friedrich. "Die Schlacht bei Gaugamela. Eine
Untersuchung zur Geschichte Alexanders d. Gr. und Ihren Quellen;
Nebst einer Beilage." Unpublished dissertation, Vereinigten
Friedrichs-Universität, 1902. Published in Halle: Buchdruckerei
von H. John, 1902. A table of contents, notes, diagrams of the
battle, comparisons of the texts of Curtius and Diodorus, of Plutarch
and Arrian and Curtius, and of Curtius and Arrian; and a vita
of the author. Henri Lebeque said of the author, "Il peut etre un
bon philogue, mais il peche par l'insuffisance des connaissances
techniques."

130 Hadjidakis, Georges N. *Du Carachère Hellénique des Anciens
Macédoniens*. Athens: Imprimerie Anestis Constantinidis, 1896.
Notes with additional sources noted in the text, and many quotations
of ancient sources which have been translated into French.

131 Hamdî, Osman *bey* and Reinach, Theodore. *Une Nécropole Royale
à Sidon*. 2 vols. Paris: E. Leroux, 1892. The first volume is called
"Texte" and the second "Plates," each with a table of contents
and illustrations; notes, and a bibliography. A valuable set by a
Turkish statesman and scholar who conducted archaeological work
at Sidon in 1887 and 1888.

132 Hampl, Franz. *Alexander der Grosse*. Persönlichkeit und
Geschichte, IX. Göttingen: Musterschmidt, [1958]. Table of
contents, diagrams, a fold-out map, and a bibliography, but no notes.
A sound and stimulating volume intended for the general reader.
The author is generally careful in his regard for the best evidence,
but views are stated rather than argued and his evidence
is not cited.

133 ——. "Der König der Makedonen." Unpublished dissertation,
University of Leipzig, 1934. Published in Weida: Druck von
Thomas and Hubert, 1934. A brief bibliography, many notes,
and a vita of the author. A new interpretation of the relations
between Alexander and the various parts of his army.

134 Hébette, Willy. "Les Connaissances Géographiques d'Alexandre le Grand." Unpublished dissertation, Université de Louvain, 1943. An expanded table of contents, many notes, 7 maps, a good bibliography, a detailed chronological table for Alexander, various tables, plates, and numerous quotations from Greek sources. An excellent volume.

*135 Hecker, Willem. *Schets Eener Inleiding op Het Leven van Alexander den Groote.* Groninger, 1857. The University of Michigan's copy is "missing."

136 Hegel, Frid. Guil. Carol. "De Aristotle et Alexandro Magno." Unpublished dissertation, Universitate Literaria Friderica Guilelma, 1837. Published in Berolini: Typis Julii Sittenfeld, 1837. Footnotes and a vita of the author.

137 Hegewisch, D[ieterich] H[ermann]. *Ueber die Griechischen Kolonieen Seit Alexander dem Grossen.* Altona: Johann Friedrich Hammerich, 1811. Table of contents, few notes with additional sources in the text, and an index. Printed in the old German type.

138 Heichelheim, Fr. *Wirtschaftliche Schwankungen der Zeit von Alexander bis Augustus.* Beiträge zur Erforschung der Wirtschaftlichen Wechsellagen Aufschwung, Krise, Stockung, Hft. 3. Jena: G. Fischer, 1930. Table of contents, graphs, various chronological tables, tables of prices, notes, and an index. The author shows a complete command of sources and of unpublished material, and his interpretations add to the value of the volume.

139 *L'Hellénisation du Monde Antique; Leçons Faites à l'École des Hautes Études Sociales* . . . . Paris: Librairie Félix Alcan, 1914. A table of contents and many notes. However, it is unfortunate that no index or bibliography was included. An excellent collection of essays by eminent historians.

140 *The Hellenistic Age; Aspects of Hellenistic Civilization,* by J. B. Bury, E. A. Barber, Edwyn Bevan, and W. W. Tarn. Cambridge: University Press, 1923. An index and many notes. The text of 4 lectures delivered at Corpus Christi College, Cambridge. A valuable and interesting summary of the results of recent research. Tarn's research had not hitherto been put before English readers in so convenient a form.

141 Helmreich, Fritz. "Die Reden bei Curtius." Unpublished
dissertation, Erlangen, 1924. Later published in Paderborn: Verlag
von Ferdinand Schöningh, 1927 as vol. XIV of *Rhetorische
Studien*. A table of contents, notes, a bibliography, and an index.

142 Hertzberg, Gustav Friedrich. *Die Asiatischen Feldzüge Alexanders
des Grossen*. 2 vols. Halle: Verlag der Buchhandlung des
Waishauses, 1864. A table of contents, notes, and an index in each
volume; also a map. A scholarly volume by a noted historian.

*143 Hess, A. *Gold Statere Alexanders d. Grossen v. Macedonien u. d.
Königs Lysimachus von Thracien Verst*. Frankfurt, 1903.
Mentioned in Sushko's *Gaugamela*.

144 Hirsch, Carl. "Beziehungen Alexanders des Grossen zu den
Griechischen Staaten," *Programm des K. K. Gymnasiums zu
Cilli am Schsusze des Schusjahres*, 1869, pp. 3-35. Quotations from
ancient sources. Printed in the old German type.

145 Hoffmann, Otto. *Die Makedonen, Ihre Sprache und Ihr Volkstum*.
Göttingen: Vandenhoeck und Ruprecht, 1906. A table of contents,
notes with additional sources in the text, indexes (place, name, and
Greek word), but no bibliography. A very useful and interesting
study that should be read by all who are interested in Greece and
her history.

146 Hoffmann, Werner. "Das Literarische Porträt Alexanders des
Grossen in Griechischen und Römischen Altertum." Unpublished
dissertation, Universität Leipzig, 1907. Later published in Leipzig:
Quelle and Meyer, 1907. Notes, an index, and a vita of the author.

147 Hogarth, David George. *Philip and Alexander of Macedon; Two
Essays in Biography*. N. Y.: Scribner's, 1897. London: J. Murray,
1897. Many notes, a list of cardinal dates in Alexander's life, a
chronology, an index, plates, and a fold-out map. An attempt to
reconstruct the characters and views of Alexander and Philip.
According to Franklin T. Richards, the author has used a fresh and
vigorous style to compress into one volume ". . . all that there is to
know about two great kings." Richards adds that the illustrations are
good and that some are new to most English readers.

148 Homo, Léon [Pol]. *Alexandre le Grand*. Paris: Librairie Arthème
     Fayard, [1951]. A table of contents, notes, an index, bibliography,
     fold-out map, and a list of the author's works. A well-written work
     rich in new observations to be read with interest and profit.
     Especially valuable for its very useful and substantial bibliography.

149 Horch, Johannes Christophorus. "Specimen Philosopho-Historicum
     de Alexandro Magni Ingenio Politico," Unpublished dissertation,
     Academia Groningana, 1836. Published in Groningana: Typis
     P. S. Barghoorn, 1836. A list of "theses" in addition to many notes.

150 Ijsewijn, J[ozef]. *De Sacerdontibus Sacerdotiisque Alexandri
     Magni et Lagidarum Eponymus*. Verhandelingen van de
     Koninklijke Vlaamse Academie voor Wetenschappen, Letteren en
     Schone Kunsten van België. Klasse der Letteren Verhandeling,
     nr. 42. Brussel: Paleis der Academiën, 1961. Many footnotes
     and an extensive bibliography. An excellent work which reaches
     many valuable conclusions.

151 Instinsky, Hans Ulrich. *Alexander der Grosse am Hellespont*.
     [Godesberg]: Küpper, [1949]. A table of contents and notes
     which are collected at the end. Because the author relied on evidence
     of public and undisputed actions, F. W. Walbank judged this
     work as an attractive, suggestive, and ". . . stimulating, but in the
     main unconvincing essay." However, A. R. Burn said that the author
     ". . . builds a strong case for holding that Alexander envisaged
     nothing less than the seizure of the whole of Asia. . . ."

152 Ivánka, Endre. *Die Aristotelische Politik und die Städtegründungen
     Alexanders des Grossen. Wege des Verkehrs und der Kulturellen
     Berührung Mit dem Orient in der Antike*. Budapest: Kir. M.
     Pázmáhy Péter Tudományegyetemi Görüg Filológiai Intézet, 1938.
     Two documented essays bound in one volume.

*153 Jacobs, W. V. *Militärisch-Philologische Untersuchungen zum
     Feldzug Alexanders Gegen die Triballer*. Münster, 1920.

154 Janke, A. "Auf Alexanders des Grossen Pfaden. Eine Reise
     durch Kleinasien." Unpublished dissertation, Universität zu Berlin,
     1904. Published in Berlin: Weidmann, 1904. Large fold-out
     colored maps, notes, a table of contents, and notes at the end. A
     useful companion to Kromayer's *Antike Schlachtfelder*. . . .

155 Jaeger, Werner. *Aristoteles; Grundlegung Einer Geschichte Seiner Entwicklung*. Berlin: Weidmannsche Buchhandlung, 1923. 2d. ed. by the same publisher in 1955. Tr. with the author's corrections and additions by Richard Robinson as *Aristotle; Fundamentals of the History of His Development*. 2d. ed. Oxford: Clarendon Press, 1948. Many notes, a general index, an index of Aristotle's works, and an index of names. An attempt to reconstruct the development of Aristotle from fragments of his works; also, an inquiry into the chronological relations of certain critical portions of his writings. By its very nature, such a volume contains much that is tentative and most controversial, but this one is to be praised for its fullness and consistency in details.

*156 Jerusalem, Wilhelm. *Alexander des Grossen Leben und Thaten*. Leipzig, 1886. The title is listed in *Kayser's Bucher-Lexikon*.

*157 Joubert, Léo. *Alexandre le Grand, Roi de Macēdoine*. Paris: Mesnil, 1889.The Newberry Library's copy is non-circulating.

158 Jouguet, Pierre. *L'Imperialisme Macedonien et l'Hellenisation de l'Orient*. Paris: La Renaissance du Livre, 1926. Rev. ed. Paris: Editions Albin Michel, 1961. Tr. by M. R. Dobie as *Macedonian Imperialism and the Hellenization of the East*. N. Y.: Knopf, 1928. Many footnotes, a table of dynasties, 4 outline maps, a full bibliography, and a good index. A discussion of the diffusion of culture resulting from the conquests of Alexander and the spread of Hellenism. The narrative is presented clearly and ably by an expert in the field. In dealing with Alexander, the emphasis is on the ideas and organization rather than on warfare. A review by W. S. Ferguson questions whether the war began with Philip's conquest of Greece rather than with Alexander.

159 ———. "Les Premiers Ptolémées et l'Hellénisation de Sarapis," *Hommages à Joseph Bidez et à Franz Cumot*. Bruxxelles: Latomus, [1949], 159-66. An annotated essay by a noted authority in the field; part of a remarkable collection.

160 Julien, Paul. "Zur Verwaltung der Satrapien unter Alexander dem Grossen." Unpublished dissertation, Universität Leipzig, 1914. Published in Weida: Druck von Thomas and Hubert, 1914. A table of contents, a name index, a geographical index, notes, a bibliography, and a vita of the author. A study of the political

organization of Alexander's empire and the extent to which it was modeled after Persian practices.

161 Jurien de la Graviere, [Jean Pierre Edmond]. *Les Campagnes d'Alexandre.* 5 vols. Paris: E. Plon, 1883-84. 2d. ed. by the same publisher in 1891. A table of contents in each volume, a portrait of the author in front of volume two, and very few notes. An interesting work written in an original style.

162 Kaerest, Julius. "Alexander der Grosse," in *Meister der Politik. Eine Weltgeschichtliche Reihe von Bildnissen,* by Erich Marcks and Karl Alexander von Müller, Berlin and Stuttgart: Deutsche Verlags-Anstalt, 1922, pp. 31-64. Printed in the old German type, this article has only 2 notes. Part of a scholarly collection of essays by authorities in each field.

*163 ———. "Beitrage zu Quellenkritik des Q. Curtius Rufus." Unpublished dissertation, Tübingen, 1878. Ordered by the Center for Research Libraries in Chicago.

164 ———. *Forschungen zur Geschichte Alexanders des Grossen.* Stuttgart: Druck und Verlag von W. Kohlhammer, 1887. Printed in the old German type; a foreword by Alfred von Gutschmid, a table of contents, notes, an examination of the text of Books V-IX of Curtius, and a comparison of texts of Curtius and Arrian and of Diodorus and Curtius. An interesting critical study that tries to determine the credibility of the official historians.

165 ———. *Geschichte des Hellenistischen Zeitalters.* 2 vols. Leipzig: Teubner, 1901. Later editions by the same publisher under the title *Geschichte des Hellenismus* in 2 vol. in 1917, 1923, 1926, and 1927. A table of contents in each volume, many notes, and an extensive listing of sources. An excellent well-known chronological study of value to the specialist as well as to the student of Hellenic history.

166 Kaiser, Wilhelm Bernhard. "Der Brief Alexanders des Grossen an Dareios nach der Schlacht bei Issos." Unpublished dissertation, Johannes Gutenberg-Universität in Mainz, 1956. Later published in Mainz: Ober-Olm, 1957. A table of contents, a vita of the author, many notes which are collected at the end, and a bibliography.

*167 Kanatsulis, D. K. "Antipatros. Ein Beitrag zur Geschichte
Makedoniens in der Zeit Philipps, Alexanders und der Diadochen."
Unpublished dissertation, Munich, 1942. Ordered by the Center
for Research Libraries in Chicago.

168 Kasten, Helmut. "Das Amnestiegesetz der Tegeaten vom Jahre 324.
Ein Beitrag zur Alexandergeschichte." Unpublished dissertation,
Hamburgischen Universität, 1922. A 3-pp. abstract was pub-
lished by the university in that same year.

169 Keller, Erich. "Alexander der Grosse nach der Schlacht bei
Issos bis zu Seiner Rückkehr aus Aegypten." Unpublished dissertation, Friedrich-Wilhelms Universität zu Berlin, 1904. Also
published in *Historischen Studien*, XLVIII (1904). Many notes
but no index or bibliography.

170 Kessler, Josef. *Isokrates und die Panhellenische Idee.* Studien
zur Geschichte und Kultur des Altertums, IV, 3. Paderborn:
F. Schöningh, 1910. A table of contents, many notes, and
comparisons of various parts of Isocrates' writings. A valuable
study which considers Isocrates a far-sighted statesman and one who
best represented the ideas which were to inspire Alexander.

171 Kirkman, Marshall Monroe. *History of Alexander the Great,
His Personality and Deeds.* Chicago: Cropley Phillips Co., 1913.
A table of contents, illustrations and a listing of them, a few
notes, an addenda with biographical notes on leading characters,
and an index.

172 Kluge, Carolus. "De Itinerario Alexandri Magni." Unpublished
dissertation, Academia Viadrina Vratislavienski Vratislaviae, 1861.
Later published in Breslau: Typis Officinae A. Neumanni,
[1861]. Notes, a chronological table with appropriate passages
from Arrian noted, list of subjects with various sources quoted,
a vita of the author, and "theses."

173 Koehler, Rudolf. "Ein Quellenkritik zur Geschichte Alexanders
des Grossen in Diodor, Curtius und Justin." Unpublished dissertation, Universität Leipzig, 1879. Published in Leipzig: Druck
von A. Haack, 1879. Few notes, a vita of the author, and no
bibliography except for sources mentioned in the preface.
Compares the texts of Curtius and Diodorus, Strabo and Diodorus,

Curtius and Arrian. Contains a number of good remarks on details and opens the question of the authority of the Alexander historians.

174 Koepp, Fr[iedrich]. *Alexander der Grosse.* "Monographien zur Weltgeschichte, IX." Bielefeld und Leipzig: Verlag von Delhagen und Klasing, 1899. Printed in the old German type with illustrations, a colored map, and an index, but no notes or bibliography. A solid work with its emphasis on philology.

175 Kohn, Josephus. "Ephemerides Rerum ab Alexandro Magno in Partibus Orientis Gestarum." Unpublished dissertation, Universitate Fridericia Guilelmia Rhenana, 1890. Published in Bonn: Typis Petri Hauptmann, 1890. Notes, sources in the text, a vita of the author, and a chronological examination of the *Ephemerides* with notes. A valuable study.

176 Kornemann, Ernst. *Die Alexandergeschichte des Königs Ptolemaios I. von Aegypten; Versuch einer Rekonstruktion.* Leipzig und Berlin: B. G. Teubner, 1935. Many notes and an index. An attempted reconstruction of Ptolemy's history (based mainly on Arrian). Kornemann tries to show that Ptolemy's work was not a mere military history but a full history; the evidence cited is not conclusive.

177 ———.*Weltgeschichte des Mittelmeer Raumes von Philipp II. von Makedonien bis Muhammed.* 2 vols. Munich: Biederstein Verlag, 1948. An expanded table of contents in each volume, fold-out maps as well as regular maps, illustrations, a list of kings by place with dates, a chronology for 2400-30 B.C. and for 27-1265 A.D., an index in vol. 2, and notes. A posthumous work which was never revised. Obviously written for the general reader. Norman H. Baynes commented that it failed to awaken his interest.

178 Korzeniewski, Dietmar. "Die Zeit des Quintus Curtius Rufus." Unpublished dissertation, Universität Köln, 1959. A table of contents, a bibliography, many notes, and a vita of the author. An excellent dissertation that surveys the history of the problem of the date of Curtius since 1841 and adds much that is significant and new.

*179 Kolalev, Sergi Ivanovich. *Aleksandr Makedonski.* Leningrad: Ogiz, 1937. The only copy in the United States is at the Library of Congress.

180 Lamartine de Prat, M. Alphonse Marie Louis. *Vie de Alexandre le Grand.* Paris: Firmin Didot Frères, 1859. A volume lacking all normal scholarly characteristics. No table of contents, index, notes, or bibliography.

181 Lamb, Harold. *Alexander of Macedon; the Journey to the World's End.* Garden City, N. Y.: Doubleday, 1946. An index, many drawings and diagrams, but no footnotes or bibliography. A map of Alexander's travels appears on the endpapers. A clear and readable portrait that is authentic history blended with imagination. According to C. A. Robinson, Jr., it is a ". . . romantic biography . . . a picture of Alexander that has little to do with reality."

182 Laudien, C. F. "Über die Quellen zur Geschichte Alexanders des Grossen in Diodor, Curtius und Plutarch." Unpublished dissertation, Universität Leipzig, 1874. Published in Königsberg: Schubert und Seidel, 1874. A table of contents, few notes, a critical discussion of the sources in the text, a comparison of the texts of Curtius and Diodorus, and a vita of the author. One of the major German studies of the period concerning the sources of the Alexander-historians.

183 Leuze, Oscar. *Die Satrapieneinteilung in Syrien und im Zweistromlande von 520-320.* Schriften der Königsberger Gelehrten Gesellschaft Geisteswissenschaftliche Klasse 11 Jahr, Heft 4. Halle (Saale): Niemeyer, 1935. An expanded table of contents, a list of abbreviations, an index, and notes. A solid contribution to the difficult problem of the satrapial organization of the Achaemenid Persians which is important for Greek and Biblical historians.

184 Lezius, Josephus. *De Alexandri Magni Expeditione Indica Quaestiones.* Dorpat: Typis Expressit C. Mattiesen, 1887. A table of contents and footnotes. A remarkable contribution which examines the sources for the history of the expedition and gives the author's views concerning them.

185 *The Life of Alexander the Great*. London: The Religious Tract Society, [1853]. A table of contents but no notes, index, or bibliography. A popularized presentation.

*186 Lilie, Fridericus. "De Onesicrito Scriptore Alexandri Magni." Unpublished dissertation, Universität Bonn, 1864. Published in Bonn: Typis Expressit Petrus Neusser, 1864.

187 Lippelt, Otto. "Die Griechischen Leichtbewaffneten bis auf Alexander den Grossen." Unpublished dissertation, Universität Jena. Later published in Weida i. Th.: Druck von Thomas and Hubert, 1910. A table of contents, notes, table of distances, general index, index of Greek words, notes, and a vita of the author.

188 Littré, [M. P.] E[mile]. *La Vérité sur la Mort d'Alexandre le Grand*. Paris: Chez René Pincebourde, 1865. A table of contents and footnotes.

189 Lorenz, Adam. *Weitere Bemerkungen über die Söldnerei bei den Griechen (von der Schlacht bei Leuktra bis zum Tode des Grossen Alexandros)*. Programm des K. Gymnasiums Eichstätt. Eichstätt: M. Däntler, 1880. Printed in the old German type, with many footnotes.

190 Lorenz, E. G. Erich. *Alexander der Grosse. Bildnis Eines Führers und Menschen*. Berlin: Verlag Reimar Hobbing, [1935]. A table of contents, a fold-out map, illustrations, but no bibliography or index, which detracts from the value of the volume.

*191 Loudet, S. M. L. *Les Rapports de l'Inde avec l'Occident, d'Alexandre à l'Empire Romain*. Paris: Dipl. ét. Sup. Fac. Lettres, 1948. The title is reviewed in the *Revue Historique* for 1949.

*192 Louvet de Couvray, A. *Les Hommes Providentiels. Alexandre, César, Napoléon*. 1865. The title is listed in the *British Museum Catalogue*.

193 M'Crindle, John Watson. *Ancient India as Described by Megasthenês and Arrian; Being a Translation of the Fragments of The Indika of Megasthenês Collected by Dr. Schwanbeck and of the First Part of the Indika of Arrian*. Calcutta: Thacker, Spink, and Co.; London: Trübner and Co., 1877. Calcutta: Chuckervertty, Chatterjee and Co., 1926. Reprinted in N. Y.: Barnes and Noble,

1969. The original edition is a reprinting with additions from the journal *Indian Antiquary* in 1876-77. Contains a map, notes, and translations of the fragments in question. This work renders a real service to students of the relations between the Orient and the Occident in antiquity.

194 ————. *The Invasion of India by Alexander the Great as Described by Arrian, Q. Curtius, Diodoros, Plutarch, and Justin.* Westminister: Archibald Constable and Co., 1893. New ed. by the same publisher in 1896. Reprinted in N. Y.: Barnes and Noble, 1969. Table of contents, illustrations, maps, bibliography, notes, general index, index of authors quoted or referred to, and a biographical appendix. An interesting and scholarly volume by an author of solid reputation.

195 McEwan, Calvin Wells. "The Oriental Origin of the Hellenistic Kingship." Unpublished dissertation, University of Chicago, 1931. Later published in Chicago: Private Edition, distributed by the University of Chicago Libraries, 1934, as part of the Oriental Institute of the University of Chicago. Studies in Ancient Oriental Civilization, no. 13. A table of contents as well as many notes. The volume's schematic account of the origin of kingship is very useful, but the author's failure to do justice to the variety of relationships and the diverse forms of ruler worship is deplored by Arthur Darby Nock.

196 Mahaffy, John Pentland. *The Progress of Hellenism in Alexander's Empire.* Chicago: University of Chicago Press, 1905. The texts of lectures delivered at the University of Chicago. Contains a table of contents, an outline for each lecture, notes and an index. The treatment is popular but the result is instructive even for the specialist.

197 ————. *The Story of Alexander's Empire.* N. Y.: Putnam's Sons, 1887. *The Progress of Hellenism of Alexander's Empire.* London: Unwin, 1905. A collection of 10 lectures delivered at a conference held at the University of Chicago, with maps, many photographs, and an index, but no footnotes or bibliography. According to Georges Radet, the volume contains a fine description of the intellectual and moral influence exercised by the Greeks; an austere publication.

198 Makowsky, Julius. "De Collatione Alexandri M. et Dindimi."
    Unpublished dissertation, Universitate Friderica Guilelma zu
    Breslau, 1919. A vita of the author, but no notes, bibliography, or
    index.

*199 Malim, Herbert. *Two Conquerors: Alexander and Caesar.*
    Bombay: Humphrey Milford, 1921. It is listed in the
    British Museum Catalogue.

200 Manen, Jan Jacob. *Penia en Ploutos in de Periode na Alexander.*
    Proefschrift. Utrecht-Zutphen: N. v. Nauta and Co., 1931.
    Notes, but other scholarly features are lacking. A useful philological
    study.

201 Marsden, E. W. *The Campaign of Gaugamela.* Liverpool:
    Liverpool University Press, 1964. Many footnotes, clear diagrams,
    an excellent map, and an index, but no bibliography. Part of the
    Liverpool Monographs on Archaeology and Oriental Studies.
    Includes discussions on the strategy of Alexander and Darius, size
    of the armies, and on the length and front of the Macedonian
    line. With original ideas the author makes a thorough attack on old
    problems in a lively and vivid style which makes for enjoyable
    and stimulating reading.

202 Maspero, Gaston Camille Charles. "Comment Alexandre Devint
    Dieu en Egypte," in his *Bibliothèque Egyptologique Contenant les
    Oeuvres des Egyptoloques Français,* XXVIII (1897), 263-86.
    Also republished in his *Études de Mythologie et d'Archeologie
    Egyptiennes.* Vol. VI. Paris: Ernest Leroux, 1912. An interesting
    article by an eminent Egyptologist, with many notes.

203 Mathieu, Georges. *Les Idées Politiques d'Isocrate.* Collection
    d'Études Anciennes. Paris: Société d'Edition "Les Belles Lettres,"
    1925. 2d. ed. by the same publisher in 1966. An expanded table of
    contents and footnotes. A study of the influence of Isocrates'
    political ideas on Philip.

204 ———. *Isocrate. Philippe et Lettres à Philippe, à Alexandre et à
    Antipatros.* Paris: E. de Boccard, 1924. A table of contents, index,
    and notes. The text of the letters, (the small type is regrettable),
    their translation into French, and the notes make this work of
    great value.

*205 Meuser, H., ed. *Das Kostüm Alexanders des Grossen.* Giessen, 1929. The title is listed in Sushko's *Gaugamela.*

*206 Meyer, Eduard. *Blüte und Niedergang des Hellenismus in Asien.* Kunst und Altertum, Alte Kulturen im Lichte Neuer Forschung, Bd. V. Leipzig: Karl Curtius, 1910. Later published in Berlin by the same publisher in 1925. An annotated volume by a recognized historian.

207 Michel, Dorothea. *Alexander als Vorbild für Pompeius, Caesar und Marcus Antonius. Archäologische Untersuchungen.* "Collection Latomus, XCIV." Brussels: Latomus, 1967. An expanded table of contents, notes, plates, a bibliography, and literature mentioned before each chapter. A valuable volume.

208 Michler, Markwart. *Die Alexandrinischen Chirurgen: Eine Sammlung und Auswertung Ihrer Fragmente.* Die Hellenische Chirurgie, No. 1. Wiesbaden: Franz Steiner Verlag, 1968. A table of contents, bibliography, index of texts cited, name index, place index, notes, and various tables.

209 Milns, R. D. *Alexander the Great.* London: Robert Hale, 1968. Illustrations, maps, diagrams, some notes, a select bibliography, and an index. According to the preface, this is an attempt to show Alexander as an "astute, ruthless and somewhat sinister political manoeuverer and manipulator of men."

210 *Miscellanea di Studi Alessandrini in Memoria di Augusto Rostagni.* Torino: Bottega d'Erasmo, 1963. A table of contents, a name index, an index of ancient sources, a list of "Elenco del Sottoscrittori," biographical information about Rostagni, and a chronological list of his works. A valuable work in honor of an eminent Hellenic philologist which contains contributions in English, French, Italian, and German.

*211 Modrzejewski, J. *Aleksander Macedoński.* Światowid Bibl. Popul.-Nauk. Warszawa: Ksiazka i Wiedza, 1958.

*212 *The Moral and Political Consequences of the Conquests of Alexander the Great.* Oxford, 1841. An anonymous work.

213 Müller, [Carl] Ludwig. *Numismatique d'Alexandre le Grand*; *suivi d'un Appendice Contenant les Monnaies de Philippe II et III et Accompagnée de Planches et Tables in Quarto*. Copenhagen: Impr. de Bianco Luno, 1855. Many footnotes, plates and tables, but no bibliography. A standard work on the Alexander coinage, cited frequently by later authors. In 1911 E. T. Newell commented that though its coverage is painstaking, the fact that the work is ". . . quite out of date and (to say the least) misleading in the majority of its attributions, has long been recognized."

214 Mueller, Carolus. *Scriptores de Rebus Alexandri Magni* printed in *Arriani Anabasis et Indica ex Optimi Codice Parisino Emendavit et Varietatem ejus Libri Retulit Fr. Dübner. Reliqua Arriani, et Scriptorum de Rebus Alexandri M*. Paris: Editore Ambrosio Firmin Didot, 1846. A collection of Greek and Latin parallel tables with an index. A remarkable collection of fragments of historians' works which existed in the time of Arrian.

215 Müller, Iwan von, ed. *Handbuch der Klassischen Altertumswis-senschaft in Systematischer Darstellung mit Besonderer Rücksicht auf Geschichte und Methodik der Einzelnen Diszipliene*. Vol. IV, section 1, part 2. *Die Griechischen Kriegsaltertumer*, by Adolf Bauer. Munchen: C. H. Beck, 1893. Many notes, plates, maps, diagrams, a very full bibliography in the text after each section, and an index of Greek and German words, names and places. A very useful handbook or manual intended for advanced students. Each part of the series has undergone many revisions to keep it as timely as possible.

216 Müller, Kurt F. "Der Leichenwagen Alexanders des Grossen." Unpublished dissertation, Universität Leipzig, 1904. Later published in Leipzig: Verlag E. A. Seemann, 1905. A double plate of the carriage, notes, diagrams, illustrations, a table of contents, and a vita of the author. An interesting thesis by one well versed in philology, archaeology, and architecture.

*217 Mussche, Herman Frank. "De Greco-Romeinse Plastiek in Westelijk Syrië en Libanon van Alexander de Grote tot Keizer Konstantijn." Unpublished dissertation, Université de Gand, 1957. Ordered by the Center for Research Libraries in Chicago.

218 Mützell, Julius, ed. *Q. Curtii Rufi de Gestis Alexandri Magni Regis Macedonum Libri Qui Supersunt Octo.* 2 vols. Berlin: Verlag von Duncker und Humbolt, 1841. A chronological table from 333-324 B.C. by month, a subject index, a name index, and various texts and codexes with notes.

219 Nachstädt, Guilelmus. "De Altera Plutarchi Declamatione quae est 'De Alexandri Fortuna'." Unpublished dissertation, Universität Berlin, 1894. Published as *Berliner Beiträge für Klassischen Philologie*, II, Berlin: Typis C. Vogtii, 1894. Notes, a Greek word index, long quotations from Plutarch with comments, and a vita of the author. A dissertation valuable for its knowledge of details about Plutarch.

220 Nadell, Jill Barbara. "Alexander and the Romans." Unpublished Ph.D. dissertation, University of Pennsylvania, 1959. An index, a bibliography, and some notes.

221 Neuffer, Eduard. "Das Kostüm Alexanders d. Gr.." Unpublished dissertation, Hessischen Ludwigs-Universität zu Giessen, 1929. A list of abbrevations, many notes collected at the end, an annotated list of evidences, and a vita of the author.

222 Niese, Benedictus. *Geschichte der Griechischen und Makedonischen Staaten Seit der Schlacht bei Chaeronea.* 3 vols. Gotha: Perthes, 1893-1903. Darmstadt Wissenschriftliche Buchgesellschaft, 1963. Many notes, a short discussion of chronology, a detailed table of contents in each volume, and an adequate and useful index for the set in the last volume. The 1963 edition is a reprint of the original. A supplement to Busolt's *Griechische Geschichte* and a companion to Hermann Schiller's *Geschichte der Pomischen Kaiserzeit.* A careful annalistic treatment of the period from one point of view— all non-political elements are practically excluded. W. S. Ferguson has criticized the set as dull and tedious, but it includes everything that happens to be available on the subject.

223 Nietzold, Walter. "Die Überlieferung der Diadochengeschichte bis zur Schlacht von Ipsos." Unpublished dissertation, Julius-Maximilians-Universität, Würzburg, 1904. Later published in Dresden: Druckerei der Neuen Verkehrs-Anstalt Hansa, 1905. An expanded table of contents, bibliography, notes, and a vita of the

author. A review by F. Reuss compliments the author on the general character of the work but expresses reservations on matters of detail.

224 Nock, Arthur Darby. *Conversion; the Old and New in Religion from Alexander the Great to Augustine of Hippo.* N. Y.: Oxford University Press, 1933; Oxford: Clarendon Press, 1933. Many notes and an index. The substance of the volume was delivered as the Lowell and the Donnellan Lectures in 1933. A discussion of the many ways in which the cults of the Mediterranean world encroached on one another. A lucid and interesting style which is not easy to read but is worth close study. The notes provide a trustworthy guide to the evidence available.

225 Oddo, Antonino. *Studi Staboniani. La Storia di Alessandri il Grande di Strabone e la Fonte di Arriano e di Plutarco.* Caltanisetta: Panfilo Castaldi, 1915. Notes and a comparison of the texts of Arrian and Strabo.

226 Oertel, [Friedrich]. *Alexander der Grosse.* Kriegsvortäge, Bd. 107. Bonn: Bonner Universitäts-Buchdruckerei, 1943. A short pamphlet containing a fold-out map and list of sources, but no notes.

227 Pagliaro, Antonino. *Alessandro Magno.* "Saggi XXXIII." Torino: Edizioni Radio-televisione Italiana, [1960]. A table of contents, a bibliography, an index, illustrations, and many notes. A scholarly volume by a professor of comparative philology at Rome University.

*228 Palau Vera, Juan. *Vidas de Grandes Hombres. Vida de Alejandro Magno, Entresacada de Plutarco, Arriano, Quinto Curtio, etc., etc.* Barcelona: G. Seix and Barral Hnos., 1930. A popular work.

229 Paribeni, Roberto. *Alessandro Magno e i Suoi Successori.* Milano: "Vita e Pensiero," 1948. A table of contents, an annotated bibliography, and a chronological table for 359-190 B.C., but few notes. According to F. W. Walbank, the volume fails to face problems and is superficial; the subject is too broad to be properly treated in a mere hundred pages.

230 ———. *La Macedonia Sino ad Alessandro Magno*. Milano: Societa Editrice "Vita e Pensiero," 1947. A table of contents, notes, and an extensive bibliography. A superficial work that fails to supplement similar works.

231 Parke, H. W. *Greek Mercenary Soldiers, from the Earliest Times to the Battle of Ipsus*. Oxford: Clarendon Press, 1933. An index, a table of principal events from 399 to 338 B.C., a table showing the number of Greek mercenaries known from 399 to 329 B.C., a list of chief authorities, and many notes. A history of the influence of mercenaries on Greek warfare which was continued by Griffith. A well-presented volume, the product of long, thorough, and painstaking study and investigation. The use of modern literature as well as ancient sources makes the volume especially useful to the scholar.

*232 Pasciucco. *Alessandro Magno ed Olimpia Complici Necessarii Nell'Uccisione di Filippo*. S. Maria Capua Vetere, 1907.

233 Pearson, Lionel Ignacius Cusack. *Lost Histories of Alexander the Great*. Philological Monograph, No. 20. N. Y.: American Philological Association, 1960. Many notes, an index, and a select bibliography. A general survey of the literary authorities for the history of Alexander and a critical and sober look at the historians. According to H. D. Westlake, "It seems that, with few exceptions, the lost histories of Alexander deserve to be lost."

234 Petersdorff, Rudolph. "Beiträge zur Geschichte Alexanders des Grossen," *Königliches Gymnasium und Real Schule I. Ordnung zu Flensburg, 1872*. (Flensburg: L. P. H. Maass, [1874]). Many notes and comparisons of the texts of various classical sources.

235 ———. "Diodorus, Curtius, Arrianus Quibus Ex Fontibus Expeditiones ab Alexandro In Asia Usque Ad Dari Mortem Factas Hauserint." Unpublished dissertation, Academia Albertina Ordinis, 1870. Published in Gedani: A. G. Kafemann, 1870. Many notes, a comparison of Arrian and Curtius, and a vita of the author.

236 ———. *Eine Neue Hauptquelle des Q. Curtius Rufus. Beiträge zur Kritik der Quellen für die Geschichte Alexanders des Grossen*. Hanover: Hahnsche Buchhandlung, 1884. A table of

contents, notes, quotations in Greek and Latin from ancient sources, and comparisons of texts of Justin and Curtius. A prudent and carefully done work.

237 Pettazzoni, Raffaele. *La Religione Nella Grecia Antica Fino ad Alessandro*. Bologna: Zanichelli, 1921. 2d ed. Turin: Einaudi, 1953. Tr. into French by Jean Gouillard as *La Religion dans la Grèce Antique, des Origines à Alexandre le Grand*. Paris: Payot, 1953. Many notes and a bibliography at the end of each chapter. The 1953 Italian edition is a reissue of the first with slight changes to the text, a new introduction, and updated bibliographies and notes. The volume contains very little that is fundamentally mistaken and displays sound judgment and a wide knowledge of facts. A review in the *Journal of Hellenic Studies* comments that this volume lacks the clarity, caution, and grasp of essentials that distinguishes Farnell's *Outline History of Greek Religion*, and that too often the author's generalities are based on disputable assumptions because he is better acquainted with theories than actual facts.

*238 Pfizer, Gustav. *Geschichte Alexanders des Grossen für die Jugend*. Stuttgart: Verlag von Sam. Gottl. Liesching, 1846. The only volume in the United States is at the New York Public Library and is not available for inter-library loan.

*239 Phrearites, Konstantinos. *History of Alex. the Great. Adaptation from Droysen from Ancient and Modern Sources*. Athens: Dionysios S. Kopida and George Gabriel, 1859. The title is listed in the *British Museum Catalogue*.

*240 Pieracconi, Dino. *Lettere del Ciclo de Alessandro in un Papiro Egiziano*. Firenze: Tip. E. Ariani, 1947.

241 Pridik, Eugen. *De Alexandri Magni Epistularum Commercio*. Berolini: Apud Speyerum et Petersium, 1893. Many notes but no index or bibliography as such—but there is a listing of 144 evidences from various contemporary sources, also a list of controversial opinions. A study of the correspondance of Alexander. An excellent volume with a complete analysis of the question. The author sees the literary tradition as authentic.

242 Radet, Georges Albert. *Alexandre le Grand*. Paris: L'Artisan
du Livre, 1931. Many notes, a bibliography following each chapter,
an index, and a fold-out map of Alexander's empire. A well-
written volume whose sources may not always be trustworthy.
C. A. Robinson, Jr., wrote in a review that the author's extreme
reconstruction has ". . . created an unhistorical and fantastic
Alexander . . . ."

243 ———. "De Coloniis a Macedonibus in Asiam cis Taurum
Deductis." Unpublished dissertation, Paris, 1892. A table of con-
tents, list of abbreviations, and notes. A very complete work.
The author visited the country before writing the dissertation.

244 ———. *Notes Critiques sur l'Histoire d'Alexandre*. Paris: E.
deBoccard; Bordeaux: Feret et Fils, 1925. A reprinting of 6 articles
which first appeared in the *Revue des Études Anciennes* without
a table of contents, bibliography, or index. There are many
footnotes. A careful analysis of the theory of Alexander's divine
world-kingdom which is very original and penetrating. However,
a review by W. W. Tarn finds the basis for Radet's arguments
to be "unfounded and improbable."

**245 ———. *Sur un Point de l'Itinéraire d'Alex. en Asie Mineure*.
1903. The title is listed in the *British Museum Catalogue*.

*246 Raeder, Anton Henrik. *Aleksander den Store*. Oslo, 1935.

*247 Raun, Carolus. "De Clitarcho, Diodori, Curtii, Justini Auctore."
Unpublished dissertation: Universität Bonn, 1868.

248 Rawlinson, George. *The Five Great Monarchies of the Ancient
Eastern World; or, the History, Geography and Antiquities of
Chaldea, Assyria, Babylon, Media, and Persia*. 3 vols. London: J.
Murray, 1862-67. 2d. rev. ed. by the same publisher in 1871.
N. Y.: Dodd, Mead and Co., 1881. Many good illustrations, a
map, notes, diagrams, and an index to scripture references. A
standard work, now badly out-of-date though still useful as the
only work containing references to all passages in Greek and
Roman literature concerning various periods of Persian and
Parthian history.

249 Reese, Wilhelm. *Die Griechischen Nachrichten über Indien bis zum Feldzuge Alexanders des Grossen. Eine Sammlung der Berichte und Ihre Untersuchung.* Leipzig: B. G. Teubner, 1914. A table of contents, notes, bibliography, and texts of fragments with a discussion of each.

250 Reichenbächer, W. "Die Geschichte der Athenischen und Makedonischen Politik vom Frieden des Philokrates bis zum Korinthischen Bund (346-338)." Unpublished dissertation, Vereinigten Friedrichs-Universität Halle-Wittenberg, 1897. Published in Halle: Druck der Buchdruckerei des Waisenhauses, 1897. Notes and a vita of the author.

251 Reinmuth, O. W. "Alexander and the World-State," *The Greek Political Experience. Studies in Honor of W. K. Prentice,* Princeton: Princeton University Press, 1941, pp.109-24. A map, index, notes, and a bibliography. One of the best brief treatments of the subject.

252 Reisch, Max. *Strasse der Zehntausend; auf den Spuren Alexanders des Grossen.* Wien: Österreichischer Bundesverlag, [1962]. A detailed chronology for 336-323 B.C., a map of Alexander's travels on the endpapers, and many illustrations with some in color. An interesting, though undocumented volume by a noted Austrian geographer, explorer, and author.

253 Reuss, Friedrich Wihelm Ludwig. "Hieronymus von Kardia." Unpublished dissertation, Marburg, 1876. Published in Marburg: Druck von C. L. Pfeil, [1876]. Notes, comparison of the texts of Hieronymus and Plutarch, and "Sententiae Controversae." A very complete work.

254 Riecke, Aemilius. "De Rebus Post Alexandri Magni Mortem Babylone Gestis Quaestionum Particula I." Unpublished dissertation, Universitate Albertina, 1887. Published in Regimonti: Leupoldiana, 1887. Notes and comparisons of Curtius and Justin. According to F. Jacoby, the volume contains a good critical examination of the sources.

255 Ritter, Hans-Werner. *Diadem und Königsherrschaft. Untersuchungen zu Zeremonien und Rechtsgrundlagen des Herrschaftsantritts bei den Persern, bei Alexander dem Grossen und im Hellenismus.* Unpublished dissertation, Universität Mainz, 1961.

Later published in Munich: C. H. Beck, 1965, as part of the
series Vestigia; Beiträge zur Alten Geschichte, Band 7. Many notes,
an index of ancient authors, a name and place index, and a good
bibliography. A badly needed volume on the history of ancient
regalia and the coronation ceremony. His arguments are well laid
out with important texts in the notes, and his conclusions are of
the greatest importance. His collection of evidence lacks only
illustrations.

256 Robinson, Charles Alexander, Jr. *Alexander the Great; the
Meeting of East and West in World Government and Brotherhood.*
1st. ed. N. Y.: E. P. Dutton, 1947. A select bibliography, an
index, and a map of Alexander's empire, but no footnotes. A biography by a classical scholar with firm foundations of exact
scholarship, which is nonetheless excellent for the general reader.

257 ———. *The Ephemerides of Alexander's Expedition.* Providence,
R. I.: Brown University Press, c1932. A map, footnotes, and a
comparison of the itineries of Arrian, Diodorus, Justin, Curtius,
and Plutarch. A scholarly study of the source material used by
the above historians. A valuable contribution to the study of Alexander; well written and attractively presented.

258 ———. *History of Alexander the Great.* 2 vols. Providence, R. I.:
Brown University Press, 1953-63. Volume one is an index to
the five existing accounts of Alexander. Volume two contains a
translation of the texts of fragments as edited by Jacoby. The
index is geographical rather than alphabetical. The endpapers contain a map of Alexander's empire. There is also an alleged
itinerary. A book for specialists who will find it extremely helpful
to have Jacoby's collection of fragments translated.

259 Robinson, Cyril Edward. *A History of Greece.* London: Methuen,
[1929]. Another edition by the same publisher in [1956].
N. Y.: Thomas Y. Crowell, [1935]. N. Y.: Barnes and Noble,
[1957]. This publisher has also reprinted the latest edition in
1960, 1962, and 1964. A table of contents, explanatory notes,
chronological tables, maps and a list of them, diagrams, illustrations
and a list of them, and an index. A brief popular presentation of
Greek history which avoids being dry or a mere cataloging of

events. The chronological tables and summaries should be invaluable to students.

260 Robson, E[dgar] Iliff. *Alexander the Great; a Biographical Study.*
London: Jonathan Cape, [1929]. A table of contents, an index,
a few notes, and a few sources which are mentioned in the preface.

261 Romains, Jules, et. al. *Alexandre le Grand.* Paris: Hachette,
1962. A collection of essays, some documented, by various authors
and containing many fine illustrations, a map of Alexander's
travels, a chronology from 357 to 323 B.C., but no index. Whereas
the volume has certain limitations common to collections—
repetition, contradiction, and omissions—it contains much that
is penetrating, learned, and is luxuriously presented.

262 Rostovtzeff, Mikhail I. *Social and Economic History of the
Hellenistic World.* 3 vols. Oxford: Clarendon Press, 1941. Plates,
a bibliography and many footnotes which are collected in Volume
three. W. W. Tarn calls the work ". . . a very great book . . . ."
Written with a standard of scholarship which can be attained only
by a select few. A standard work by a truly monumental historian.

263 Roussel, Pierre. *La Grèce et l'Orient des Guerres Médiques à la
Conquête Romaine.* Peuples et Civilisations, II. Paris: F. Alcan,
1928. 2d. ed. by the same publisher in 1938. An expanded table of
contents, 2 maps, an index, and a bibliography in the first note
of each section, but few other notes. An exact and concise work
of solid scholarship.

264 Ruegg, August. "Beiträge zur Erforschung der Quellenverhält-
nisse in der Alexandergeschichte des Curtius." Unpublished
dissertation, Universität Basel, 1906. Published in Basel: Buchdruckerei Emil Birkhauser, 1906. A table of contents, a bibliography,
notes, comparison of the texts of Diodorus and Arrian and a
vita of the author. According to F. Reuss, the work is characterized
by much insight but unacceptable hypotheses.

265 Rüstow, Wilhelm and Köchly, H. A. T. *Geschichte des Griechischen
Kriegswesens von der Ältesten zeit bis auf Pyrrhos.* Uarau:
Verlags-Comptoir, 1852. Printed in the old German type; many
notes, illustrations, diagrams, and fold-out maps. An excellent
study of war by a professional military man.

266 Russell, Ada. *Alexander the Great.* N. Y.: Frederick A. Stokes
Co., [c1914]. A table of contents, plates (some colored), a
fold-out map, illustration list, and an annotated list of sources,
but no notes.

267 St. John, Bayle. *Adventures in the Libyan Desert and the Oasis of
Jupiter Ammon.* London: J. Murray, 1849. N. Y.: G. P. Putnam's
Sons, 1849. An expanded table of contents and notes, but no
bibliography or index. An interesting volume written in a polished
style.

268 [Sainte Croix, Guillaume Emmanuel Joseph Guilhem de Clermont-
Lodève, *baron* de]. *Examen Critique des Anciens Historiens
d'Alexandre-le-Grande.* Paris: Imprimerie de Delance et Lesueur,
1775. Later editions by the same publisher in 1804 and 1810.
Tr. from the French by Sir Richard Clayton as *A Critical Inquiry
into the Life of Alexander the Great.* Bath: G. G. and J. Robinson,
1793. A table of contents, a chronological table for 360 to 317
B.C., illustrations, an index of authors, a general index, 2 large
fold-out maps, notes, tables, and many quotations from ancient
sources. The volume was first published as an essay and then later
expanded. The bibliography is exhaustive and annotated. A volume
of value and interest to all Alexander-historians and students
of Alexander.

*269 San Nicolò, Mariano. *Ein Babylonischer Sklavenkaufvertrag aus
der Zeit Alexanders d. Grossen.* 1930. The title is listed in the
British Museum Catalogue.

270 Savill, Agnes Forbes. *Alexander the Great and His Time.* London:
Rockliff, 1955. 2d ed. by the same publisher in 1959. 3d. ed.
N. Y.: Citadel Press, 1966. The second edition was revised and
sections were rewritten, errors corrected, and a fold-out map was
added. Contains illustrations, a bibliography, a list of important
dates, an index, and few notes. A volume written with enthusiasm
and yet easy to read. A volume of interest especially for its
treatment of Alexander's medical condition.

271 Schachermeyr, Fritz. *Alexander der Grosse; Ingenium und Macht.*
Graz: Anton Pustet, 1949. Many plates, a fold-out map, a bibliography, many footnotes, but no index. Called ". . . the best of the

Alexanders thus far . . ." by C. B. Welles. A comprehensive biography with an attractive narrative style.

272 Schnabel, Paul. *Berossos und die Babylonisch-Hellenistische Literatur*. Leipzig: B. G. Teubner, 1923. A table of contents, various tables, a list of abbreviations, but no notes—sources are noted in the text. The fact that the fragments of Berosus are given without commentary is to be regretted. But the author's conclusions are very interesting, and for this reason, the volume is of value to the scholar.

*273 Schneider, R. *Olympias, die Mutter Alexanders des Grossen*. Zwiekau, 1885.

*274 Schoenborn, A. *Der Zug Alexanders durch Lycien*. Posen: W. Decker and Co., 1848.

275 Schoene, Alfredus. *Analecta Philologica Historica. I. De Rerum Alexandri Magni Scriptorum, Imprimis Arriani et Plutarchi, Fortibus*. Leipzig: B. G. Teubner, 1870. A short undocumented pamphlet. A few sources are mentioned in the text. Contains comparisons of texts of Arrian and Plutarch and of Arrian and Diodorus.

276 Schrader, Rudolf. "De Alexandri Magni Vitae Tempore." Unpublished dissertation, Bonn, 1889. A vita of the author and many notes.

277 Schreiber, Theodor. *Studien über das Bildniss Alexanders Grossen. Ein Beitrag zur Alexandrinischen Kunstgeschichte Mit einem Anhang über die Anfänge des Alexanderkultes*. Leipzig: B. G. Teubner, 1903. A table of contents, notes, plates and illustrations, a list of museums by country and city with the art piece located there and the page in the text where it is mentioned. An elaborate analysis of the portraits of Alexander which classifies them under 25 types.

278 Schroeter, Fridericus. "De Regum Hellenisticorum Epistulis in Lapidibus Servatis Quaestiones Stilisticae." Unpublished dissertation, Universität Lipsiae, 1931. Published in Lipsiae: B. G. Teubner, 1931. A table of contents, notes, a brief bibliography, a table of comparative citations as they appear in various collections

of inscriptions, and a vita of the author. The reproduction in toto
of 65 letters and 22 fragments makes the work extremely valuable.

279 Schubart, Wilhelm. *Ägypten von Alexander dem Grossen bis
auf Mohammed.* Berlin: Weidmann, 1922. A table of contents,
illustrations, map, chronological table from 336 B.C. to 640/1
A.D., map, index, but no notes. A general survey of life in Egypt
by a noted Egyptologist; printed in the old German type.

280 Schubert, Rudolf. *Beiträge zur Kritik der Alexanderhistoriker.*
Leipzig: Dieterich'sche Verlagsbuchhandlung M. B. H., 1922. A
table of contents, no notes, but sources are mentioned in the
text. A supplement to his *Die Quellen zur Geschichte der Diodo-
chenzeit* (1914). A collection of 3 essays which is a useful
commentary on some of the problems connected with the ancient
sources.

281 ———. *Die Quellen zur Geschichte der Diadochenzeit.* Leipzig:
Dieterich'sche Verlagsbuchhandlung Theodor Weicher, 1914.
A table of contents and an index; there are no notes, but sources
are mentioned in the text.

282 Schulze-Gävernitz, Ruth von. "Astronomisch-Geographische
Nachrichten der Alexanderhistoriker aus Indien." Unpublished
dissertation, Ruprecht-Karls-Universität zu Heidelberg, 1927.
Published in Berlin: Emil Ebering, 1927. A table of contents,
notes, and a vita of the author.

283 Schwartzenfeldt, Joachim von [Stülpnagel, Joachim von].
Alexander, Herr der Welt. Stuttgart: Franckh, [1957]. Many
illustrations, a chronological table from 370 to 323 B.C., and
explanation of some terms, a map on the endpapers, but no footnotes
or bibliography. An elementary book (on the high school level)
by a retired army officer.

284 Schwarz, Franz von. *Alexanders des Grossen Feldzüge in Turkestan.
Geschichtswerken des Flavius Arrianus und Q. Curtius Rufus
auf Grund Vieljähriger Reisen im Russischen Turkestan und den
Angrenzenden Ländern.* Munich: E. Wolff, 1893. 2d. ed. Stuttgart:
Fr. Grub Verlag, 1906. A table of contents, 7 maps, illustrations,
tables, and a few notes. An excellent commentary on Arrian
and Curtius.

285 Scott, [Sir James] George. *Peeps at Great Explorers. Alexander the Great*. London: A. and C. Black, Ltd., 1928. A table of contents, illustrations, and a map, but no index, bibliography, or notes. A popular presentation.

286 Sghedoni, A. M. *Alessandro il Grand*. Torino: Società Editrice Internazionale, [1956]. Table of contents, illustrations, but no notes—a popularized presentation.

287 Snyder, John W. *Alexander the Great*. N. Y.: Twayne Publications, [c1966]. Maps, a chronology, notes, and references, an index, and a good selected annotated bibliography. A capable and balanced report whose style is occasionally dense but worth reading. E. A. Fredricksmeyer does not consider this work a serious scholarly contribution, and he judges it idealized since it is based largely on Tarn.

288 Sordi, Marta. *La Lega Tessala Fino ad Alessandro Magno*. Istituto Italiano per la Storia Antica, Rome. Studi, no. 15. Roma: Istituto Italiano per la Storia Antica, 1958. An expanded table of contents and an index. A well balanced volume with much that is new. A new interpretation of the Thessalian Confederacy by one of the leading scholars in the field. A provocative book of considerable merit.

289 Spak, Isaac. "Der Bericht des Josephus über Alexander den Grossen." Unpublished dissertation, Albertus-Universität zu Königsberg, 1911. Published in Konigsberg: Hartungsche Buchdruckerei, 1911. Many notes and a vita of the author. A criticism of the testimony of Josephus concerning Alexander.

290 Stark, Freya. *Alexander's Path, from Caria to Cilicia*. London: J. Murray, 1958; N. Y.: Harcourt, Brace, 1958. Many Illustrations, a map, many footnotes, and a bibliography. A travel volume concerning the geography of the area and a reconstruction of Alexander's campaigns and marches.

291 ———. *The Lycian Shore*. N. Y.: Harcourt, Brace, [1956]; London: J. Murray, [1956]. Many illustrations, maps, an index, and a bibliography. A beautifully written and illustrated travel book about a journey along the Asia Minor coast of present day Turkey as once travelled by Alexander.

292 Stein, Mark Aurel. *On Alexander's Track to the Indus; Personal Narrative of Explorations on the North-West Frontier of India, Carried Out Under the Orders of H. M. Indian Government by Sir Aurel Stein.* London: Macmillan and Co., Ltd., 1929. Many illustrations, maps, and an index, but no footnotes or bibliography. The narrative of a voyage following the steps of Alexander as far as possible. A volume of great interest and charm.

293 Strasburger, Hermann. *Ptolemaios und Alexander.* Leipzig: Dieterich, 1934. The text and a discussion of Arrian book by book, a table of contents, a bibliography with additional sources in the text, but no notes. A source-index to the *Anabasis* by one who possesses the philological skill and historical knowledge to make this a useful study. While intended as a brief introduction to, or analysis of, Arrian, much is directed toward Ptolemy. According to F. Jacoby, most of the commentary is accurate and perceptive, though some statements are disputed. George Mathieu agrees that the results need further examination and non-German sources need to be checked.

294 Susemihl, Franz. *Geschichte der Griechischen Literatur in der Alexandrinerzeit.* 2 vols. Leipzig, 1891-92. Hildesheim: G. Olds, 1965. Many notes, an alphabetical index by A. Brunk, an expanded table of contents, but no bibliography. A complete and connected history of Greek literature in a readable and well-written text with elaborate and learned notes. The 1965 edition is a reprint of the original.

295 Sushko, Alexander. *Gaugamela, the Modern Qaraqosh.* Series Historico-Philologica, IX. Chicago: Academia Scientarum Ucrainica Americana, 1936. An expanded table of contents, illustrations, maps, notes, and an extensive bibliography. A scholarly work notable for its excellent bibliography.

296 Sykes, Percy Molesworth. *Ten Thousand Miles to Persia or Eight Years in Irán.* N. Y.: Charles Scribner's Sons, 1902; London: J. Murray, 1902. A good fold-out map, a table of contents, a list of illustrations, diagrams, notes, and an index. The record of extensive travels in Persia by the British consul. The volume contains too few references to authorities, and it reflects the author's leanings

toward the British upper class and imperialism. A well-written, popularized account for the general reader.

297 Tänner, Kurt. "Das Verpflegungswesen der Griechischen Heere bis ander d. Gr." Unpublished dissertation, Universität Jena, 1912. Published in Jena: Frommannsche Buchdruckerei (Hermann Pohle), 1912. A table of contents, notes, an index, and a vita of the author.

*298 Tanner, James Gosset. *Four Notable Men: Oliver Cromwell, Erasmus, Alexander the Great, Cardinal Newman*. London: Charles J. Thynne, 1912. The title is listed in the *British Museum Catalogue*.

299 Tarn, William Woodthrope. *Alexander the Great*. 2 vols. Cambridge: University Press, 1948. Vol. I reprinted in Boston: Beacon Press, 1956. Volume one contains an enlargement of his chapters in *Cambridge Ancient History*; Volume two contains a series of essays discussing the problems and sources of the Alexander story. This set, by one of the greatest authorities on the Hellenistic world, has been judged as a most important work by such scholars as Bikermann, Heichelheim, A. H. M. Jones, and C. H. Robinson, Jr. The first volume will appeal to the general reader, the second will be indispensable to the scholar.

300 ———. *The Greeks in Bactria and India*. Cambridge: University Press, 1938. Later editions by the same publisher in 1951 and 1966. Many plates, maps, notes, an index, but lacks a bibliography. The second edition is a reprint of the first with a 20-pp. addenda in which the author answers some criticisms of the first edition and notes recent publications, especially numismatic. The volume is of great value to the scholar because of its critical examination of all evidence which is put into usable shape.

301 ———. *Hellenistic Civilization*. London: E. Arnold, 1927. Later editions by the same publisher in 1930, 1952, and 1959. Cleveland: World Publishing Co., 1961. Many notes, maps, an index, and a list of general works. The third edition contains maps for the first time—with the collaboration of G. T. Griffith. A stimulating and well-documented volume which has long been recognized as without rival in its field.

302 ———. *Hellenistic Military and Naval Developments*. Cambridge: University Press, 1930. N. Y.: Biblo and Tannen, 1966. Many footnotes and an index. The 1966 edition is a reprint of the 1930 volume. The republication with amplifications and notes of his Lees-Knowles Lectures for 1929-30. A just and scholarly classical military history by an eminent historian.

303 Telschow, Kurt. "Die Griechischen Flüchtlinge und Verbannten von der Archaischen Zeit bis zum Restitutionsedikt Alexanders des Grossen (324)." Unpublished dissertation, Christian-Albrechts-Universität zu Kiel, 1952. A table of contents, bibliography, notes, and margin guides.

304 Thonke, Willy. "Die Karte des Eratosthenes und die Züge Alexanders." Unpublished dissertation, Kaiser-Wilhelms Universität zu Strassburg i. E., 1914. Published in Strassburg: i. E.: Druckerei der Strassburger Neusten Nachrichten A.-G., 1914. Notes and a vita of the author.

305 Tritsch, Walther. *Olympias. Die Mutter Alexanders des Grossen*. Frankfurt: Societäts-Verlag, [1936]. A table of contents, bibliography, maps, chronology from 2000 to 310 B.C., family tree, and illustrations, but no notes.

*306 *Two Cities [viz. Edessa and Merv] in Their Relation to the Life of Alexander the Great*. Hampstead, 1904. The Yale University Library's copy is non-circulating.

307 Ujfalvy, Charles de. *Le Type Physique d'Alexandre le Grand d'après les Auteurs Anciens et les Documents Iconographiques*. Paris: Albert Fontemoing, 1902. A table of contents, notes, and many plates and a list of them. It is divided into two parts: authors of antiquity and modern times, and iconographic documents. An excellent volume enhanced by its many fine illustrations.

308 Val'dgauer, Oskar Ferdinandovich. "Ueber einige Porträts Alexanders des Grossen." Unpublished dissertation, Kgl. Ludwig-Maximilians-Universität zu Munchen, 1903. Published in Munich: Kgl. Hofbuchdruckerei Kastner und Callwey, 1903. Notes and a vita of the author.

309 Valmin, [Mattias]Natan. *Alexander der Store: Världsfredens Förste Förkämpe.* Stockholm: Natur och Kultur, 1942. A table of contents and illustrations, but it lacks notes, bibliography, and index. A popularized account by a Swedish scholar.

310 Vezin, August. "Eumenes von Kardia." Unpublished dissertation, Universität zu Tübingen, 1907. Notes, a bibliography (in a note), and a vita of the author. Wilhelm Schubart, Henri Lebegue, and Martens praise the author for his knowledge of the subject, his good judgment, and his style.

311 Vietta, Egon [Fritz, Egon]. *Alexander Scheitert an Indien; auf den Spuren Alexanders vom Punjab bis Istambul.* Bern: Francke, [1957]. A series of essays with plates, but there are neither footnotes nor a bibliography.

312 Vincent, William. *Voyage de Néarque, des Bouches de l'Indus jusqu'à l'Euphrate, ou Journal de l'Expédition de la Flotte d'Alexandre, Rédigé sur le Journal Original de Néarque Conservé par Arrian, à l'Aide des Eclaircissemens Puisés dans les Écrits et Relations des Auteurs, Geographes, ou Voyageurs, Tant Anciens que Modernes; et Contenant l'Historie de la Première Navigation que des Européens Aient Tentée dan la Mer des Indes.* Tr. from the English by J. B. L. S. Bille. Paris: l'Imprimerie de la Republique, 1800. Fold-out maps, index, tables, and margin notes.

313 Vogel, Theodor. *Q. Curti Rufi Historiarum Alexandri Magni Macedonis Libri Qui Supersunt.* Berlin: Weidmann, 1867. 2 vols. Leipzig: B. G. Teubner, 1875-80. Later edition by the same publisher in 1903-06. Text of Arrian with the author's notes.

314 Volkmann, Didericus, ed. "Itinerarum Alexandri," in *Einlandungs-Program zu der am 22 Mai 1871 Stattfindenden Drei Hundert und Achtundzwanzigsten Stiftungsfeier der Königlichen Landesschule Pforta* (Naumburg: Heinrich Seiling, 1871). Many footnotes and an index.

315 Weber, Franz. "Alexander der Grosse im Urteil der Greichen und Römer bis in die Konstantinische Zeit." Unpublished dissertation, Universität Giessen, 1909. Published in Borna-Leipzig: Buchdruckerei Robert Noske, 1909. A table of contents, an annotated

chronological list of classical authors, notes, a location index for classical sources mentioned in this work, and a vita of the author.

*316 Weber, L. *De Plutarcho Alexandri Imitatore.* Halle: Genethliacon Gottingense, 1888. It is reviewed in the 1890 edition of *Revue de Philologie.*

317 Weigall, Arthur Edward Pearse Brome. *Alexander the Great.* N. Y. and London: G. P. Putnam's Sons, 1933. Garden City, N. Y.: Garden City Publishing Co., [1936]. Many footnotes and an index but no bibliography. William MacDonald called this work a ". . . rare combination of learning and literary skill, a contribution to history . . . ." But C. A. Robinson, Jr. said that the author employed ". . . the very negation of historical scholarship . . . . He has given us neither Alexander nor the Alexander of romance."

318 Welles, Charles Bradford. *Royal Correspondence in the Hellenistic Period; A study in Greek Epigraphy.* New Haven, Conn.: Yale University Press, 1934. A table of contents, a "list of works cited by abbreviated title," a "comparative table of editions," a list of texts, various indexes, illustrations, notes, and the Greek texts of the inscriptions with English translations. A valuable and scholarly work—a study in philology and historical interpretation. The English translations of the 75 texts are extremely welcome.

319 Wenger, Franz. "Die Alexandergeschichte des Aristobul von Kassandrea." Unpublished dissertation, Julius-Maximilianus Universität, 1914. Published in Ansbach: G. Brügel and Son, 1914. Printed in the old German type; notes, a vita of the author, comparisons of the texts of Arrian and Strabo and of Diordorus and Arrian, and a discussion of the *Anabasis,* book by book.

*320 Westermann, Ant. *De Alexandri M. Epistolis.* 1852. The title is listed in Engelmann's *Bibliotheca Scriptorum Classicorum.*

321 Wheeler, Benjamin Ide. *Alexander the Great; the Meeting of East and West in Universal History.* N. Y.: G. P. Putnam's Sons, 1900. Many illustrations and maps, footnotes, and an extensive index. The major part of this volume appeared in *Century Magazine* (Vol. LVII and LVIII), the last 9 articles with the text substantially unchanged. One of the best popular histories of Alexander, written by an expert scholar with power and charm.

322 Wheeler, Mortimer. *Flames Over Persepolis*; *Turning-Point in
     History*. London: Weidenfeld and Nicolson, [1968]. Table
     of contents, illustrations (some color), diagrams, maps, notes, and
     index. A study of the spread of Alexander's influence east of
     Iran with a complete archaeological survey by a British archaeolo-
     gist and authority on ancient India.

323 Wilamowitz-Moellendorff, Ulrich von. *Der Glaube der Hellenen*.
     2 vols. Berlin: Weidmannsche Buchhandlung, 1931-32. Basel:
     Benno Schwabe, 1956 and [1959]. Many notes, a name and
     place index, an index of classical sources, and a modern author
     index. An admirable work displaying great learning by an eminent
     scholar. The second volume was assembled after the author's
     death and edited with care by Gunther Keakkenbach; it was well
     indexed by Hiller von Gartringen. Because of the numerous
     allusions to works of other scholars and because the reader is often
     left to draw his own conclusions, its primary appeal and value
     will be for those specialists who have some knowledge of the
     subject.

324 Wilcken, Ulrich. *Alexander der Grosse*. Leipzig: Quelle und
     Meyer, 1931. Tr. as *Alexander the Great* by G. C. Richards. N. Y.:
     Dial, 1932. Available in paperback by Norton, 1967. Many
     footnotes, a good bibliography, fold-out map, and index. The
     notes and bibliography in the 1967 edition were updated by
     Eugene Borza. A brilliant piece of work based on an investigation
     of the original authorities and on modern discoveries. When it
     was first published, C. A. Robinson, Jr. called it the best modern
     biography of Alexander; admirably translated.

325 Will, Édouard. *Histoire Politique du Monde* Hellénistique
     (*323-30 av. J. C.*). 2 vol. Nancy. Université. Faculté des Lettres
     et des Sciences Humaines, Memoire n° 30 and 32. Nancy:
     Faculté des Lettres et des Sciences Humaines de l'Université de
     Nancy, 1966-67. A table of contents, a list of principal abbrevia-
     tions, a general bibliography and one after each section, and an
     index to the set in the second volume. A clear, detailed account of
     the political history of the Hellenistic period and a summary of
     the scholarship on the subject over the past sixty years. Truesdell S.
     Brown calls this a work of interpretation with its critically an-
     notated narrative and critical bibliographical discussions.

326 Williams, John. *The Life and Actions of Alexander the Great*.
London: J. Murray, 1828. Later editions by the same publisher in
1829 and 1860. N. Y.: J. and J. Harper, 1831. Later published
as *The Life of Alexander the Great*. N. Y.: Perkins Books Co.,
[c1902]. A fold-out map but no footnotes or bibliography. A
popularized account written with strength and freedom of style.

327 ————. *Two Essays on the Geography of Ancient Asia; Intended
Partly to Illustrate the Campaigns of Alexander, and the Anabasis
of Xenophon*. London: John Murray, 1829. Notes and 3 fold-out
maps. A collection and comparison of the details of marches and
itineraries. An able and convincing accumulation of knowledge.

*328 Winter, Franz. *Das Alexandermosaik aus Pompeii*. Strassburg:
Schlesier und Schweikhardt, 1909. Non-circulating at all United
States locations.

329 Woodcock, George. *The Greeks in India*. London: Faber and Faber,
1966. Plates, maps, a bibliography, but no notes. A useful guide
for the general reader which summarizes the vast literature
available. A continuous narrative which for the first time includes
the entire first millennium during which the Greeks were known in
India. A stimulating and clear study of cultural contacts between
India and the classical world which may exaggerate the continuity
and extent of Greek cultural influence.

330 Wright, Frederick Adam. *Alexander the Great*. London: Routledge
and Sons, 1934. N. Y.: McBride, 1935. Many plates, a map of
Alexander's empire, an index, very few footnotes, and no
bibliography. An unqualified eulogy which regards Alexander as
almost above criticism; not concerned with a critical consideration
of the sources. Intended for the general reader.

331 Wulff, Oskar. *Alexander Mit der Lanze. Eine Bronzstatuette der
Sammlung der Herrn A. v. Nelidow*. Berlin: Verlag von
A. Asher and Co., 1898. A useful work with illustrations and notes
which are collected at the end.

332 Yorck von Wartenburg, Hans David Ludwig. *Kurze Übersicht der
Feldzüge Alexanders des Grossen*. Berlin: Ernst and Siegfried
Mittler and Son, 1897. A table of contents, bibliography, many

maps, tables, and a few notes. A very good work on military history by a modern military specialist.

333 Zama, Cezar. *Historia dos Trés Grandes Capitães da Antiguidade.* 2 vols. Bahia: Livaria Progresso Editora, [1893]. No notes, bibliography, index, or table of contents. Reprint of various articles by a statesman which appeared in the *Jornal do Commercio.*

334 Zancan, Paola. *Il Monarcato Ellenistico nei Suoi Elementi Feder-ativi.* Padua. Università. Facoltà di Lettere e Filosofia. Pub-blicazioni, VII. Padova, 1934. A table of contents and notes. An excellent volume for the specialist interested in the relationships between the Hellenistic monarchy and its various elements.

*335 Zhebelev, S. A. *Aleksandr Velikii.* Berlin: 1922. The Yale University Library copy is "non-circulating."

336 Zogheb, Alexandre Max de. *Le Tombeau d'Alexandre le Grand et le Tombeau de Cléopâtre.* Paris: Ernest Leroux, 1896. An interesting, documented volume.

337 Zolling, Th. *Alexanders des Grossen Feldzüg in Central-Asien. Ein Quellenstudie.* Leipzig: Verlag von Johann Friedrich Hart-knoch, 1875. Chronological tables, notes, a comparative table of texts of Arrian, Curtius, and Diodorus on various subjects. A useful study by one who is acquainted with the ancient literature.

338 Zumetikos, Alexander M. "De Alexandri Olympiadisque Epistularum Fontibus et Reliquiis." Unpublished dissertation, Friderica Guilelma Universität, 1894. Published in Berlin: Apud Mayerum et Muellerum, 1894. An expanded table of contents, notes, and a vita of the author. An excellent volume containing a complete view and analysis of sources concerning the corres-pondence of Alexander.

B. Serials

1 Aalders, G. J. D. "Xenophon als Voorloper van het Hellenisme," *Tijdschrift voor Geschiedenis,* LXIV (1951), 368-75.

2 Abbot, James. "Addendum on the Battlefield of Alexander and Porus," *Asiatic Society of Bengal, Calcutta. Journal,* XVIII (1849), 176-77.

3 ————. "Gradus ad Aornon," *Asiatic Society of Bengal, Calcutta. Journal,* VII (1854), 309-63. Illustrations, notes, comparisons in English of the texts of Arrian and Curtius, and a comparative table showing various versions of Alexander's route.

4 ————. "Some Account of the Battle Field of Alexander and Porus," *Asiatic Society of Bengal, Calcutta. Journal,* XVII (1848), 619-33. A fold-out map.

5 ————. "Some Account of the Camps and Battlefield of Alexander and Porus," *Asiatic Society of Bengal, Calcutta. Journal, XVIII* (1849), 619-33.

6 Abel, F.-M. "Alexandre le Grand en Syrie et en Palestine," *Revue Biblique,* XLIII (1934), 528-45 and LXIV (1935), 42-61.

7 Adcock, Frank Ezra. "Greek and Macedonian Kingship," *British Academy for the Promotion of Historical, Philosophical, and Philological Studies. Proceedings,* XXXIX (1953), 163-80. Text of the Raleigh Lecture on History read May 20, 1953, with notes added.

Unless otherwise noted, all periodical articles are adequately documented. Only exceptional qualities (pictures, diagrams, maps, bibliographies, etc.) will be indicated.

8 ———. "Sir William Woodthrope Tarn, 1869-1957," *British Academy for the Promotion of Historical, Philosophical, and Philological Studies. Proceedings*, XLIV (1958), 253-62. A plate, but no footnotes.

9 Albrechtsen, Erling. "Aleksander den Stores Visitkort," *KUML*; *Aarbog for Jysk Arkaeologisk Selskab. Aarhaus*, 1958, pp. 172-89. A map, diagrams, and many illustrations, but few notes. Pages 186 to 189 are an English translation entitled, "Alexander the Great's Visiting Card."

10 ———. "Alexander the Great's Visiting Card," *Illustrated London News*, XXVII (Aug. 27, 1960), 351-53. Many photographs and a map, but cites no sources and lacks footnotes.

11 "Alexander," *Knight's Penny Magazine*," VIII (1839), 133-34, 141-43, 158-60. One illustration and a few notes, but no sources are given.

12 Alföldi, Andreas. "Die Ausgestaltung des Monarchischen Zeremoniells am Römischen Kaiserhofe," *Deutsches Archaologisches Institut. Romische Abteilung. Mitteilungen*, XLIX (1934), 1-111. A table of contents as well as notes.

13 Alfonsi, Luigi. "Pompeo in Manilio," *Latomus*, VI (1947), 345-51. A comparison of the personalities of Alexander and Pompey.

14 Alsina Clota, Jose. "La Religión Helenística (Génesis y Caracteres)," *Helmantica. Revista de Humanidades Clasicas*, VI (1955), 387-418. A critical bibliography.

15 Altheim, Franz. "Alexander und Zarathustra," *Gymnasium*, LVIII (1951), 123-29. No footnotes, but sources are listed in the text and at the end of the article.

16 Altheim, Franz and Stiehl, Ruth. "Alexander the Great and the Avesta," *East and West*, VIII (1957), 123-35.

17 ———. "Die Araber Zwischen Alexander und Mohammed," *Altertum*, VIII (1962), 102-113. One map and one note listing sources.

18 Anderson, Andrew Runni. "Alexander at the Caspian Gates," *American Philological Association. Transactions,* LIX (1928), 130-63. A list of authors who refer to the Caspian Gates in classical literature; also quotations from Josephus.

19 ———. "Bucephalas and His Legend," *American Journal of Philology,* LI (1930), 1-21. Quotations from ancient sources.

20 Andréadès, A. "'Ai Spoudaióterai 'epì Alexándrou toû M. Dēmosiou 'Omoiai," *Akadēmia Athenōn. Praketika,* IV (1929), 231-42.

21 ———. "Les Finances de Guerre d'Alexandre le Grand," *Annales d'Histoire Economique et Sociale,* I (1929), 321-333. A listing of troops by country.

22 Andreotti, Roberto. "Per una Critica dell'Ideologia di Alessandro Magno," *Historia,* V (1956), 257-302.

23 ———. "Il Problema di Alessandro Magno nella Storiografica dell'Ultimo Decennio," *Historia,* I (1950), 583-600. Many footnotes listing an exceptional number of sources.

24 ———. "Die Weltmonarchie Alexanders des Grossen in Überlieferung und Geschichtlicher Wirklichkeit," *Saeculum,* VIII (1957), 120-66. An extensive bibliography in addition to its many footnotes.

25 Anspach, Aug[ust] Ed[uard]. "De Alexandri Magni Expeditione Indica," *Wisserschaftliche Beilage zum Programm des Königlich Gymnasiums zu Duisburg, Ostern,* 1901-03, pp. 1-131. Many footnotes but no index or bibliography.

26 "Aornos," *Great Britain and the East,* XXIX (June 30, 1926), 760-61. An undocumented article.

27 Arnim, H[ans] v[on]. "Zur Entstehungsgeschichte der Aristotelischen Politik," *Akademie der Wissenschaften, Wien. Philosophisches-Historische Klasse. Sitzungsberichte,* CC (1924), 1-130. Few notes but additional sources are mentioned in the text; also there are quotations from ancient sources.

28 Atkinson, J. E. "Primary Sources and the Alexanderreich," *Acta Classica*, VI (1963), 125-37. The substance of a paper presented before the Classical Association of South Africa Conference in Pietermaritzburg, February, 1963.

29 Austin, F. B. "A Saga of the Sword," *Saturday Evening Post*, CXCIX (Feb. 26, 1927), 18-19, 54-59. An undocumented article with drawings by H. J. Joulen.

*30 Aymard, André. "Basileùs Makedónōn," *Mélanges Fernand de Visscher*, III (1950). Reviewed in *Revue Internationale des Droits de l'Antiquité*, II (1949).

31 ———. "Un Ordre d'Alexandre," *Revue des Études Anciennes*, XXXIX (1937), 5-28. An abstract appears in the *American Journal of Archaeology*, XLI (1937), 613.

32 ———. "Le Protocole Royal Grec et son Évolution," *Revue des Études Anciennes*, L (1948), 232-63.

33 ———. "Les Sarcophages de Sidon au Musée de Constantinople," *Revue Bleue*, L (1892), 118-20.

34 ———. "Sur l'Assemblée Macédonienne," *Revue des Études Anciennes*, LII (1950), 115-37.

35 ———. "Sur Quelques Vers d'Euripide qui Poussèrent Alexandre au Meutre," *Brussels. Université Libre. Institut de Philologie et d'Histoire Orientales et Slaves. Annuaire*, IX (1949), 43-74.

36 Babelon, E. "La Stylis Attribut Naval sur les Monnaies," *Revue Numismatique*, 4th. ser., XI (1907), 1-39. Two plates and a table of diagrams used on coins.

37 Babelon, Jean. *"Alexandre le Grand au Cabinet des Médailles," Demareteion; Numismatique-Glyptique-Archeologie-Haute Curiosité*, I (1935), 113-16. Photographs; sources noted in the text.

38 Badian, E. "The Administration of the Empire," *Greece and Rome*, XII (1965), 166-82.

39 ———. "Agis III," *Hermes; Zeitschrift für Klassische Philologie*, XLV (1967), 170-92. A brief bibliography and an appendix on the date of Agis' war.

40 ———. "Alexander the Great and the Creation of an Empire," *History Today*, VIII (1958), 369-76 and 494-502. Few footnotes but many photographs and a map of Alexander's travels.

41 ———. "Alexander the Great and the Loneliness of Power," *A.U.M.L.A.*, XVII (1962), 80-91. The text of a lecture with notes appended.

42 ———. "Alexander the Great and the Unity of Mankind," *Historia*, VII (1958), 425-44. A comparison (in English) of the texts of Erathosthenes and Plutarch.

43 ———. "Ancient Alexandria," *History Today*, X (1960), 779-87. Many photographs and a map; no footnotes.

44 ———. "The Date of Clitarchus," *African Classical Association. Proceedings*, VIII (1965), 5-11.

45 ———. "The Death of Philip II," *Phoenix*, XVII (1963), 244-50.

46 ———. "Egypt Under the Ptolemies," *History Today*, X (1960), 451-59. Many photographs; no footnotes.

47 ———. "The Eunuch Bagoas; A Study in Method," *Classical Quarterly*, n.s., VIII (1958), 145-57.

48 ———. "First Flight of Harpalus," *Historia*, IX (1960), 245-46.

49 ———. "Harpalus," *Journal of Hellenic Studies*, LXXXI (1961), 16-43. An extraordinary number of notes.

50 ———. "Orientals in Alexander's Army," *Journal of Hellenic Studies*, LXXXV (1965), 160-61. A comment on Brunt's and Griffith's article concerning Alexander's cavalry (*J.H.S.* LXXXIII [1963], 27).

51 Balsdon, J. P. V. D. "The 'Divinity' of Alexander," *Historia*, I (1950), 363-88.

52 Bardolff, Carl Frhr. v. "Der Siegeszug Alexanders des Grossen nach dem Osten," *Gymnasium*, 1942, pp. 27-42. A colored fold-out diagram; few footnotes.

53 Bardon, H. "Quinte-Curce," *Les Études Classiques*, XV (1947),
    3-14, 120-37, and 193-220 (as "La Valeur Littéraire de
    Quinte-Curce). Latin and Greek quotations; additional sources
    listed in the text.

54 Barker, Ernest. "The Life of Aristotle and the Composition and
    Structure of the *Politics*," *Classical Review*, XLV (1931), 162-72.

55 Bauer, Adolf. "Der Brief Alexanders des Grossen über die Schlacht
    gegen Porus," *Festgaben zu Ehren Max Büdinger's von seinen
    Freuden und Schülern* (Innsbruck, 1898), pp. 69-88. Few notes;
    sources are cited in the text.

56 ————. "Erste Abtheilung. Abhandlungen. Der Todestag Alexan-
    ders des Grossen," *Zeitschrift für die Österreichischen Gymnasien*,
    XLII (1891), 1-13. A comparison of the texts of Arrian and
    Plutarch.

57 ————. "Die Schlacht bei Issos," *Oesterreichisches Archäologisches
    Institut in Wien. Jahreshefte*, II (1899), 105-28. Drawings
    and two maps.

58 Bauer, Adolf and Strzygowski, Josef. "Eine Alexandrinische
    Weltchronik; Text und Miniaturen eines Griechischen Papyrus
    der Sammlung W. Goleniščev," *Denkschriften der Wiener
    Akademie, Philosophisch-Historische Klasse*, LI, abhandlung
    2 (1906), 1-204. Many plates and drawings of Greek papyri with
    a discussion of variations in text.

59 Bellinger, Alfred R. "An Alexander Hoard from Byblos," *Berytus;
    Archeological Studies*, X (1950/51), 37-49. A catalog of coins
    arranged systematically by mint; plates of coins; a list of the works
    of E. T. Newell on this subject; one note.

60 Benedikt, Ernst. "Alexander the Great," *Contemporary Review*,
    CXCIII (Apr., 1958), 181-84. No footnotes.

61 Bengtson, Hermann. "Alexander und der Hellenismus; Ein
    Forschungsbericht über Neuerscheinungen," *Welt als Geschichte*,
    IV (1939), 168-87.

62 ———. "Philoxenos 'O Makedōn; Ein Beitrag zur Verwaltungs-geschichte 'Ioniens,' Insbesondere im Alexanderreich," *Philologus*, XCII (1937), 126-55.

63 ———. Untitled. *Gnomon*, XIII (1937), 113-29. A documented discussion of Oskar Leize's *Die Satrapieneinteilung in Syrien und im Zweistromlande von 520-320.*

64 Berve, Helmut. "Alexander; Versuch einer Skizze Seiner Entwick-lung," *Die Antike*, III (1927), 128-45. No footnotes and no sources.

65 ———. "Die Angebliche Begründung des Hellenistichen Königs-kultes durch Alexander," *Klio; Beiträge zur Alen Geschichte*, XX (1926), 179-86. A comparison of the texts of Plutarch and Arrian.

66 ———. "Das Geographische Weltbild Alexanders des Grossen," *Forschungen und Fortschritte; Korrespondenzblatt der Deutschen Wissenschaft und Technik*, XVIII (1942), 185-86.

67 ———. "Ulrich Wilcken: Alexanders zug an die Oase Siwa," *Gnomon*, V (1929), 370-86. A documented discussion of Wilcken's *Alexander the Great.*

68 ———. "Die Verschmelzungspolitik Alexanders des Grossen," *Klio; Beiträge zur Alten Geschichte*, XXXI (1938), 135-68.

69 Bevan, Edwyn Robert. "The Deification of Kings in Greek Cities," *English Historical Review*, XVI (1901), 625-39.

70 Bickerman, E. J. "A Propos d'un Passage de Mytilène," *Parola del Passato; Rivista di Studi Classici*, XVIII (1963), 241-55. Greek quotations and a comparison of two versions of Chares; photographs.

71 Bickermann, E[lias]. "Alexandre le Grand et les Villes d'Asie," *Revue des Études Grecques*, XLVII (1934), 346-74. Also published as a pamphlet in Paris by Ernest Leroux in 1934.

*72 Bidez, Joseph. "Les Écoles Chaldéennes sous Alexandre et les Séleucides," in *Mélanges Capart* (1935). The title is listed in Tarn's *Hellenistic Civilization.*

73 Bieber, Margarete. "Ein Idealisiertes Porträt Alexanders des Grossen," *Deutsches Archäologisches Institut. Jahrbuch,* XL (1925), 167-82. Many photographs.

74 ———. "A Late Roman Portrait Head of Alexander the Great in Boston," *American Journal of Archaeology,* 2d. ser., XLIX (1945), 425-29. Two views of the head and several views of coins.

75 ———. "The Portraits of Alexander the Great," *American Philosophical Society. Proceedings,* XCIII (no. 5) (1949), 373-427. Many plates; sources cited in the text in addition to those in footnotes.

76 ———. "The Portraits of Alexander," *Greece and Rome,* 2d. ser, XII (1965), 183-88. Many illustrations.

77 Bielawski, Jozef and Plezia, Marian. "Zachowany w. Jezyku Arabskim Memoriał Arystotlesa do Aleksandra Wielkoego z Roku 330 p.n.e.," *Polska Akademia Nauk. Wydzial I. Nauk Spolecznych. Sprawozdania z Prac Naukowych,* VI(2) (1963), 12-17. No notes, but sources are mentioned in the text.

78 Biezuńska-Malowist, Iza. "Aleksander Macedoński-C. Iulius Caesar," *Meander; Miesięcznik, Poświęcony Kulturze Świata Starozytnego,* III(2) (1948), 116-18. Two illustrations; no notes.

79 Bikerman, E. "Diagramma," *Revue de Philologie,* XIV (ser. 3, vol. XI) (1937), 295-312. Quotations in Greek from ancient sources.

80 ———. "L'Europeanisation de l'Orient Classique; A Propos du Livre de Michel Rostovtzeff," *Renaissance,* II (1944-45), 381-92.

81 ———. "La Lettre d'Alexandre le Grand aux Bannis Grecs," *Revue des Études Anciennes,* XLII (1940), 25-35.

82 Blum, Gustave. "Contribution à l'Imagerie d'Alexandre," *Revue Archéologique,* II (1911), 290-96. Two views of a bust of Alexander.

83 Blümmer, Franz. "Alexander der Grosse, der Sohn des Jupiter Ammon," *Programm des Grossherzoglischen Gymnasiums*

zu Büdingen als Einladung zu der am 6. April 1868 (Büdingen: Andr Heller, 1868). Quotations in Greek from ancient sources.

84 Bois, Henri. "Alexandre le Grand et les Juifs en Palestine," *Revue de Théologie et de Philosophie*, XXIII (1890), 557-80; XXIV (1891), 78-98.

85 Borza, Eugene N. "Alexander and the Return from Siwah," *Historia*, XVI (1967), 369. No footnotes, but sources are mentioned in the text.

86 Bourguet, Émile. "Inscriptions de Delphes," *Bulletin de Correspondance Hellénique*, XXIII (1899), 486-510. A reproduction of an inscription and a re-setting in Greek script.

87 ———. "Les Inscriptions de Delphes," *Revue Archéologique*, 5th. ser., VII (1918), 209-51. Quotations from Greek inscriptions.

88 ———. "Les Inscriptions de Delphes et M. Pomtow," *Revue Archéologique*, 4th. ser., XXIII (1914), 413-24.

*89 Boyunaga, Y. "Alexandre le Grand d'après les Sources Orientales," *Pinar* (Istanbul), I(1) (1960), 9-11; I(2) (1960), 7-8.

90 Breccia, Evaristo. "II Diritto Dinastico Nelle Monarchie dei Successori d'Alessandro Magno," *Studi di Storia Antica*, IV (1903), 1-167. A detailed table of contents, Greek quotations, a chronology of rulers by place, and a table of dynasties by place with surname and nickname.

91 ———. "L'Eredità di Alessandro Magno e l'Impero Romano," *Pisa. Scuola Normale Superiore. Annali. Lettere, Storia e Filosofia*, 2d. ser. II (1933), 53-67. Text of a speech given at the Accademico dell'Universita di Pisa on Nov. 19, 1932; no notes.

92 ———. "Wilcken, Ulrich—Alexanders Zug an die Oase Siwa (Sonderabdruck aus den Sitzungsberichten der Preussischen Akademie der Wissenschaften. Phil.-Hist. Klasse 1928, XXX, p. 30)," *Societé Archéologique d'Alexandrie. Bulletin*, XXV (1930), 152-61. A documented discussion of a passage in Wilcken's article.

93 Brown, Truesdell S. "Alexander's Book Order (Plut. Alex. 8)," *Historia*, XVI (1967), 359-68.

94 ———. "Callisthenes and Alexander," *American Journal of Philology*, LXX (1949), 225-48.

95 ———. "Clitarchus," *American Journal of Philology*, LXXI (1950), 134-55.

96 ———. "Hieronymus of Cardia," *American Historical Review*, LII (1946-47), 684-96.

97 ———. "A Megasthenes Fragment on Alexander and Mandanis," *American Oriental Society. Journal*, LXXX (1960), 133-35.

98 Bruhl, Adrien. "Le Souvenir d'Alexandre le Grand et les Romains," *École Française de Rome. Mélanges d'Archéologie et d'Histoire*, XLVII (1930), 202-21. Illustrations.

99 Brunt, P. A. "The Aims of Alexander," *Greece and Rome*, 2d. ser., XII (1965), 205-15.

100 ———. "Alexander's Macedonian Cavalry," *Journal of Hellenic Studies*, LXXXIII (1963), 27-46. Two tables: the number of forces by country that crossed with Alexander, and the totals for his army as given by various ancient sources.

101 ———. "Persian Accounts of Alexander's Campaigns," *Classical Quarterly*, n.s., XII (1962), 141-55.

102 Buchler, Adolphe. "La Relation de Josèphe Concernant Alexandre le Grand," *Revue des Études Juives*, XXXVI (1898), 1-26.

103 Buchner, Edmund. "Zwei Gutachten für die Behandlung der Barbaren durch Alexander den Grossen?," *Hermes; Zeitschrift für Klassische Philologie*, LXXXII (1954), 378-84.

104 Bunbury, Edward H. "Additional Tetradrachms of Alexander the Great," *Numismatic Chronicle and Journal of the Royal Numismatic Society*, 3d. ser., III (1883), 1-17. Plates and word descriptions of coins.

105 ———. "On Some Unpublished Tetradrachms of Alexander the Great," *Numismatic Chronicle and Journal of the Royal*

Numismatic Society, n.s., VIII (1868), 309-20. Contains word descriptions of coins and a table of coin weights.

106 Burn, A. R. "The Generalship of Alexander," *Greece and Rome*, 2d. ser., XII (1965), 140-54.

107 ———."Notes on Alexander's Campaigns, 332-330," *Journal of Hellenic Studies*, LXXII (1952), 81-91. A chronology for the date of Gaugamela and a diagram of Alexander's right wing.

108 Burr, Victor. "Das Geographische Weltbild Alexanders des Grossen," *Würzburger Jahrbücher für die Altertumswissenschaft*, II (1947), 91-99.

109 Burton, R. G. "Alexander the Great and the Indian Frontier," *Edinburgh Review*, CCL (July, 1929), 50-64. No footnotes, although a few sources are mentioned in the text. At first glance appears to be a review of Stein's *On Alexander's Track to the Indus*, but in reality is a discussion of Stein's trip through the area and Alexander's connection to it.

110 Byvanck, A. W. "La Bataille d'Alexandre," *Vereeniging tot Bevordering der Kennis van de Antike Beschaving*, XXX (1955), 28-34. Many plates and a chronology of monuments from 375 to 295 B.C.

111 "Cailloux, Pousse." "The Silver Hand of Alexander," *Golden Book Magazine*, VIII (1928), 310-20. An undocumented article.

112 Carrata Thomes Franco. "Il Problema degli Eteri nella Macedonia di Alessandro Magno," *Turin. Università. Facoltà di Lettere e Filosofia. Pubblicazioni*, VII (1955), fasc. 4, 1-59. A table of contents, an index of classical sources, a name index, quotations in Greek from classical sources, a discussion of the texts of various classical authors by book and line, and an alphabetical list of classical sources.

113 Cavaignac, E. "A Propos de la Bataille d'Alexandre Contre Porus," *Journal Asiatique*; *Recueil de Memoires et Notices Relatifs aux Études Orientales*, CCIII (Oct.-Dec., 1923), 332-34. No footnotes, but sources are mentioned in the text.

114 Cauer, Friedrich. "Philotas, Kleitos, Kallisthenes. Beiträge zur Geschichte Alexanders des Grossen," *Neue Jahrbucher für Philologie und Padagogik. Neue Folge der Supplemente Band,"* XX (1893), 1-79. Quotations from Greek sources. Sources are cited in the text in addition to footnotes.

115 Chapot, Victor. "Alexandre Fondateur de Villes (simples réflexions)," *Mélanges Gustave Glotz* (Paris: Les Presses Universitaires de France, 1932), 173-81.

116 Chaumeix, André. "Deux Portraits de l'Époque Hellénistique," *Ecole Française de Rome. Mélanges d'Archéologie et d'Historie,* XIX (1899), 91-100. Some illustrations.

117 Chinnock, E. J. "The Burial-Place of Alexander the Great," *Classical Review,* VII (1893), 245-46. A collection of passages from ancient sources translated into English.

118 Chroust, A.-H. "Was Aristotle Actually the Preceptor of Alexander the Great?," *Classical Folia,* XVIII (1964), 26-33.

119 Clark, L. Pierce. "Unconscious Motives Underlying the Personalities of Great Statesmen and their Relation to Epoch-Making Events. III. The Narcism of Alexander the Great," *Psychoanalytic Review,* X (1923), 56-69.

120 Cloché, Paul. "La Grèce de 346 à 339 av. J.-C.," *Bulletin de Correspondance Hellénique,* XLIV (1920), 108-59.

121 Cohen, D. "Annotationes ad Auctores et Papyros Nonnullas," *Mnemosyne,* n.s., LIV (1926), 81-87.

122 Colombini, Arrigo. "Per una Valutazione dei Rapporti Delfico-Macedoni dalle Origini del Regno Argeade ad Alessandro Magno," *Studi Classici e Orientali,* XII (1963), 183-206. Quotations in Greek from ancient sources.

123 Corssen, P. "Das Angebliche Werk des Olynthiers Kallisthenes über Alexander den Grossen," *Philologus,* LXXIV (1917), 1-57.

124 Corte, Matteo Della. "L'Educazione di Alessandro Magno nell'Enciclopedia Aristotelica in un Trittico Megalografico di Pompei del II Stile," *Deutsches Archäologisches Institut. Römische Abteilung. Mitteilungen,* LVII (1942),

31-77. Many drawings, a plan of the "Casa del Criptoportico" in Pompeii, and pictures of frescoes on the walls.

125 Costanzi, Vincenzo. "L'Eredità Politica d'Alessandro Magno," *Annali delle Università Toscane*, n.s., III (1918), no. 2. A table of contents, a brief bibliography with a list of abbreviations, notes, and quotations in Greek from ancient sources.

126 Court, M. A. "Collection of Facts Which May Be Useful for the Comprehension of Alexander the Great's Exploits on the Western Banks of the Indus (with map)," *Asiatic Society of Bengal, Calcutta. Journal*, VIII (1839), 304-13.

127 Couve, L. and Bourguet, E. "Inscriptions Inédites du Mur Polygonal de Delphes," *Bulletin de Correspondance Hellénique*, XVII (1893), 343-409. The texts of the inscriptions, index of proper names in Greek; no notes.

128 Creasy, Professor. "(From Bentley's Miscellany for January) The Imperial Four. Alexander, Caesar, Charlemagne, and Napoleon," *Eclectic Magazine of Foreign Literature, Science and Art*, XXVIII (1853), 306-11, 477-81.

129 ———. "The Imperial Four. Alexander, Caesar, Charlemagne and Napoleon," *Eclectic Magazine of Foreign Literature, Science, and Art*, XXIX (1853), 162-67.

130 Crönert, Wilhelm. "Griechische Literarische Papyri aus Strassburg, Freiburg und Berlin," *Akademie der Wissenschaften, Gottingen. Nachrichten*, 1922, pp. 1-46. A graphic representation of the papyri in Greek.

131 Cumont, Fr. "Alexandre Mourant ou Mithra Tauroctone?," *Revue Archéologique*, 6th. ser., XXVII (1947), 5-9. Many views of various statues.

132 Cunningham, A. "Coins of Alexander's Successors in the East," *Numismatic Chronicle and Journal of the Royal Asiatic Society*, VIII (1868), 93-136, 181-213, 257-83; IX (1869), 28-46, 121-53, 217-46, 293-318; X (1870), 64-90, 205-36. Many plates and drawings of coins, quotations in Greek from ancient sources, a word description of coins, various tables (letters and symbols,

"Conjectural family connexion of the Greek princes of Bactriana, Ariana, and India").

133 Dahlmann, Hellfried. "Studien zu Senecas Consolato ad Polybium. IV. Die Zeit des Curtius Rufus," *Hermes; Zeitschrift für Klassische Philologie*, LXXII (1937), 311-16.

134 Dascalakis, Apostolos. "La Déification d'Alexandre le Grand en Égypte et la Réaction en Grèce," *Studii Clasice. Bucharest*, IX (1967), 93-105. See also entry 135.

135 Daskalakis, Ap. B. " 'E Theopoiēsis toû Megalou 'Alexandrou Kai tà Schedia Ellnoas latines 'Auto Kratorias," *Athens. Ethnikon Panepistemion. Epistemonike Epeteris*, X (1959-60), 35-179.

136 ————. "La Jeunesse d'Alexandre et l'Enseignement d'Aristotle," *Studii Clasice*, VII (1965), 169-80.

137 Davis, Elmer. "What Price Supermen? The Sad Case of Alexander the Great," *World Today*, LIV (1929), 537-42. An undocumented article.

138 Dechambre, A. "Carachères des Figures d'Alexandre le Grand et de Zénon le Stoïcien Éclairés par la Médecine," *Revue Archéologique*, ser. 1, Year IX, (1852) (2), 422-40. An extract of a lecture read at the Academie des Beaux-Arts on May 22, 1851. Some illustrations.

139 Delbrueck, Richard. "Der Spätantike Kaiserornat," *Antike; Zeitschrift für Kunst und Kultur des Klassischen Altertums*, VIII (1932), 1-21. No notes; many plates.

140 DeSanctis, Gaetano. "Gli Ultimi Messaggi Alessandro ai Greci," *Rivista di Filologia*, LXVIII (n.s., XVIII) (1940), 1-21.

141 Deonna, Waldemar. "Le Noeud Gordien," *Revue des Études Grecques*, XXXI (1918), 39-81, 141-83. Many illustrations.

142 Dieterich, Karl. "Alexander der Grosse im Volksglauben von Griechen, Slaven und Orientalen," *Allegemeine Zeitung. Beilage*, CLXXXIV (1904), 289-92. Printed in the old German type.

143 Dieulafoy, Marcel Auguste. "La Bataille d'Issus," *Academie des Inscriptions et Belles-Lettres, Paris. Memoires*, XXXIX (1914), 41-76. A colored fold-out map.

144 Domaszewski, Alfred v. "Die Phalagen Alexanders und Caesars Legionen," *Carl Winter's Sitzungsberichte der Heidelberger Akademie der Wissenschaften. Philosophisch-Historische Klasse*, XXV (Jan., 1926), 3-86.

145 Droysen, Johann Gustav. "Alexander des Grossen Armee," *Hermes; Zeitschrift für Klassische Philologie*, XII (1877), 226-52. A table showing the size of Alexander's army as reported by various ancient sources; also a table showing troops by their home country.

146 ———. "Alexander des Grossen züge durch Turán," *Rheinisches Museum für Philologie*, II (1834), 81-102. Printed in the old German type.

147 ———. "Beiträge zu Frage über die Innere Gestaltung des Reiches Alexanders des Grossen," *Akademie der Wissenschaften, Berlin. Monatsberichte*, 1877, pp. 23-45. Quotations from ancient sources.

148 ———. "Beiträge zu der Frage über die Innere Gestaltung des Reiches Alexanders des Grossen," in his *Kleine Schriften zur Alten Geschichte*, II (Leipzig: Viet and Co., 1894), 232-52.

149 Droysen, Joh. Gust. "Zu Duris und Hieronymos," *Hermes; Zeitschrift für Klassische Philologie*, XI (1876), 458-65. No notes, but sources are mentioned in the text.

150 ———. "Zur Geschichte der Nachfolger Alexanders," *Rheinisches Museum für Philologie*, II (1843), 387-414, 511-30. Various tables and quotations in Greek from classical sources. Printed in the old German type.

151 Duchalais, A. "Monnaies Frappées en Commun par les Villes de Phères, d'Atrax, d'Argissa, de Castanea et des Athamans," *Revue Numismatique*, 1853, pp. 255-76. A plate, word descriptions of coins by place, and quotations from ancient Latin and Greek sources.

152 Dussaud, René. "L'Ère d'Alexandre le Grand en Phénicie
    (336 avant J.-C.)," *Revue Numismatique*, 1908, pp. 445-54.
    Many photographs of coins.

153 "Echos et Nouvelles. Societe Toulousaine d'Etudes Classiques,"
    *Toulouse. Université. Bulletin de l'Université et de l' Académie
    de Toulouse*, XLV (March, 1936), 179-81. No notes.

154 Eddy, Mary Garvin. "Sarcophagi in the Attic," *Aramco World
    Magazine*, XX(2) (Mar.-Apr. 1969), 30-32. No notes and one
    color photograph.

155 *Edinburgh Review*. "History of Greece. By George Grote, Esq.
    Vol. XII. London: 1856," *Edinburgh Review*, CV (1857), 305-41.
    A documented essay concerning Grote's *History of Greece*;
    also quotations in Greek from ancient sources.

156 *Edinburgh Review*. "Two Essays on the Geography of Ancient
    Asia: Intended Partly to Illustrate the Campaigns of Alexander,
    and the Anabasis of Xenophon. By the Rev. John Williams,"
    Edinburch Review, LIII (1831), 306-28. A documented essay
    concerning Williams' work.

157 Egger, Emile. "Aristotle Considéré Comme Précepteur d'Alexandre
    le Grand," *Journal des Savants*, Feb. 1861. Reprinted in *Mémoires
    de Littérature Ancienne*, 1862, pp. 444-60, with several changes.

158 Eggermont, P. H. L. "Indica. Indië en de Hellenistische Rijken.
    Hun Onderlinge Verhouding in de Eerste Eeuw Na den Dood
    van Alexander den Grooten," *Vooraziatische-Egyptisch Gezelschap
    "Ex Orientale Lux,"* VIII (1942), 735-46. A map in addition
    to its notes.

159 Ehrenberg, Victor "Ost und West. 'Alexander der Grosse,' "
    Prague. Deutsche Universität. Philosophische Fakultät. Schriften,
    XV (1935), 140-76. No notes.

160 ———. "Polypragmosyne: A Study in Greek Politics,"
    Journal of Hellenic Studies, LXVII (1947), 46-67.

161 Ehrhardt, A. A. T. "Jesus Christ and Alexander the Great,"
    Journal of Theological Studies, XLVI (1945), 45-51. Comparisons

of texts of Plutarch and Philippians in Greek with an English translation.

162 Emerson, Alfred. "The Portraiture of Alexander the Great: a Terracotta Head in Munich," *American Journal of Archaeology*, II (1886), 408-13; III (1887), 234-60.

163 Endres, Heinrich. "Krateros, Perdikkas, und die Letzten Pläne Alexanders; eine Studie zu Diod. XVII 4, 1-6," *Rheinisches Museum für Philologie*, LXXII (1917/18), 437-45.

164 Ensslin, W. "Die Gewaltenteilung im Reichsregiment nach Alexanders Tod," *Rheinisches Museum für Philologie*, LXXIV (1925), 293-307. Quotations from ancient Greek literature; also a comparison of Arrian and Justin.

165 Erzen, Afif. "Büyük Iskenderle III. Darius Arasindaki Issos Muharebesinin Mevkii Hakkinda," *Türk Tarih Kongresi*, IV (1952), 59-66.

166 Esser, A. Albert M. "Hatte Alexander der Grosse Heterchrome Augen?," *Klinische Monatsblätter* für Augenheilkunde, LXXXIV (1930), 704-06. A brief bibliography.

167 Eussner, A. "Römische Historiker der Kaiserzeit. Erster Artikel. Q. Curtius Rufus," *Philologus*, XXXII (1873), 157-78. A bibliography in the text, few notes, and a table of codices.

168 "The Expedition of Alexander to the Oasis of Jupiter Ammon," *Tait's Edinburgh Magazine*, n.s., XVI (1849), 228-32. An undocumented account of St. John's *Adventures in the Lybian Desert* and related works. Also in *Eclectic Magazine of Foreign Literature, Science and Art*, XVII (1849), 277-82.

169 Fakhry, Ahmed. "A Temple of Alexander the Great at Bahria Oasis," *Egypt. Ministry of Foreign Affairs. Service des Antiquites. Annales*, XL (1940-41), 823-28. A plan of the temple.

170 Farnell, L. R. "Hellenistic Ruler-Cult: Interpretation of Two Texts," *Journal of Hellenic Studies*, XLIX (1929), 79-81. A sparsely documented clarification of two texts used by Tarn in his article, "The Hellenistic Ruler-Cult and the Daemon,"

JHS, XLVIII (1928), 206. Followed by a note from Tarn stating that he is unconvinced by the new interpretation.

171 Favez, Charles. "Alexandre le Grand Vu par Sénèque," *Palaeologia. Kodaigaku,* VII (1958), 107-110.

172 Fazy, Robert. "La Prise de l'Aornos par Alexandre le Grand en 326 avant J.-C.," *Mélanges d'Histoire et de Littérature Offerts à Monsieur Charles Gilliard à l'Occasion de son Soixante-Cinquième Anniversaire* (Lausanne: Rouge-Publ. de la Fac. des Lettres de Lausanne, 1944), pp. 7-16. A two-page map and many notes.

173 Ferguson, W. S. "Athenian Politics in the Early Third Century," *Klio; Beiträge zur Alten Geschichte,* V (1905), 155-79.

174 Ferrabino, Aldo. "Una Lezione su Alessandro Magno," *Annali della Istruzione Media,* VI (1930), 151-62.

175 Festugière, A.-J. "Trois Recontres Entre la Grèce et l'Inde," *Revue de L'Histoire des Religions,* CXXV (1943), 32-57.

176 Fick, Richard. "Die Buddhistische Kultur und das Erbe Alexanders des Grossen," *Morgenland; Darstellungen aus Geschichte und Kultur des Ostens,* XXV (1933), 1-41. An entire issue containing many drawings and photographs; notes collected at the end of the issue; and a brief bibliography.

177 Fies, Oswald. "Die Geburt Alexanders des Grossen. (Die Wandlung einer Geburtsgeschichte)," *Sudhoffs Archiv für Geschichte der Medizin und der Naturwissenschaften,* XI (1918/9), 260-77. Résumés of various versions of the birth.

178 Filliozat, Jean. "Alexandre et l'Inde," *Information Historique,* 1947, pp. 142-43.

179 Fisch, M. H. "Alexander and the Stoics," *American Journal of Philology,* LVIII (1937), 59-82 and 129-51. A comparison of Tarn's *Alexander the Great* and his previous works. Three appendices: 1.) notes on Erwin R. Goodenough's, "The Political Philosophy of Hellenistic Kingship," in *Yale Classical Studies,* I (1928), 55-102; 2) a discussion of "The Stoic *Oikeiosis* Doctrine;" 3) notes on Johannes Stroux's "Die Stoische Beurteilung

Alexanders des Grossen," *Philologus*, LXXXVIII (1933), 222-40.

180 Fontana, Maria Josè. "Il Problema delle Fonti per Il XVII Libro di Diodoro Siculo," *Kokalos*, I (1955), 155-90. Greek and Latin quotations, also comparisons of Diodorus and Cleitarchus.

181 Foucart, P. "Inscriptions d'Asie Mineure," *Bulletin de Correspondance Hellénique*, IX (1885), 387-403. The texts of the inscriptions in Greek.

182 ———. "Inscriptions d'Orchomène," *Bulletin de Correspondance Hellénique*, III (1879), 452-65. The texts of inscriptions in Greek.

183 Foucher, A. "Les Satrapies Orientales de l'Empire Achéménide," *Academie des Inscriptions et Belles Lettres, Paris. Comptes Rendus des Seances*, 1938, pp. 336-52. A table of satraps and a map.

184 Fraser, P. M. "Alexander and the Rhodian Constitution," *La Parola del Passato; Rivista di Studi Classici*, VII (1952), 192-206. Many quotations in Greek from ancient sources.

185 Frederichsmeyer, Ernest A. "Alexander, Midas, and the Oracle at Gordium," *Classical Philology*, LVI (1961), 160-68. This article was summarized in the *American Journal of Archaeology*, 2d. ser., LXIV (1960), 184.

186 ———. "The Ancestral Rites of Alexander the Great," *Classical Philology*, LXI (1966), 179-82. An examination of a letter from Olympias to Alexander.

187 Furtwängler, A. "Ancient Sculptures at Chatsworth House," *Journal of Hellenic Studies*, XXI (1901), 214-28. Many illustrative plates.

188 Gaevernitz, Ruth v. S. "Aristotle, Alexander and the Idea of Mankind," *Contemporary Review*, CCV (Oct., 1964), 543-48.

189 Gagé, Jean. "Hercule-Melquart, Alexandre et les Romains à Gades," *Revue des Etudes Anciennes*, XLI (1940), pp. 425-38.

190 Gallet de Santerre, H. "Alexandre le Grand et Kymé d'Éolide," *Bulletin de Correspondance Hellénique*, LXXI-LXXII (1947-48), 302-06.

191 Gebauer, Kurt. "Alexanderbildnis und Alexandertypus," *Deutsches Archäologisches Institut. Athenische Abteilung. Mitteilungen*, LXIII-LXIV (1938-39), 1-106. A list of Alexander art objects and plates of some of them; also a long bibliography.

192 Geier, Robert. "De Ptolemaei Lagidae Vita et Commentariorum Fragmentis Commentatio," *Ad Scholae Latinae in Orphanotropheno Halensi Examen Sollemne de V. Menis Aprilis Anni MDCCCXXXVIII* (Hallis: Saxonum, 1838), 1-76. Date guides in the margins, a family tree, and quotations in Greek from ancient sources.

193 ————. "Ueber Erziehung und Unterricht Alexanders des Grossen," in *Programm der Lateinischen Hauptschule zu Halle für das Schuljahr* 1847-48 (Halle: Eduard Anton, 1848). Printed in the old German type.

194 Geiger, Wilhelm. "Alexanders Feldzüge in Sogdiana," *Programm der Studienanstalt zu Neustadt a.dH. für des Schuljahr 1883/84*, 1884, pp. 3-46. Many quotations from Greek sources.

195 Gerassimov, Th. "The Alexandrine Tetradrachms of Cabyle in Thrace," *American Numismatic Society. Centennial Publications*, 1958, pp. 273-77. Plates of the coins.

196 Gercke, Alfred. "Alexandrinische Studien (Fortsetzung)," *Rheinisches Museum für Philologie*, XLII (1887), 590-626. Contains tables comparing the texts of Kallimachos and Theokritas; also, a chronological table for them for the years 324/3-230.

197 Ghislanzone, Ettore. "Gli Scavi delle Terme Romane a Cirene. 17. Statua Colossale di Alessandro il Grande," *Notiziario Archeologico*, II (1916), 105-22. Illustrations.

198 Gitti, Alberto. "Alessandro Magno e Il Reponso di Ammone," *Rivista Storica Italiana*, LXIV (1952), 531-47.

*199 ————. "Quando nacque in Aless. Magno l'Idea della Filiazione Divina," *Accademia Pugliese delle Scienze, Bari. Classe di Sc. Mor. Atti e Realizioni*, n.s., III-IV (1950-51), 1-39. It is listed in the *l'Annee Philologique*, vol. XXII-XXIII.

200 ————. "L'Unitarietà della Tradizione su Alessandro Magno nella Ricerca Moderna," *Althenaeum*, XXXIV (1956), 39-57.

201 Gjurić, M. N. "Aleksandar Makedonski Kao Ekumenski Kosmotvorats (Alexander the Great as an Oecumenical Cosmothetist)," *Ziva Antika; Antiquite Vivante*, IV (1954), 16-59. Written in Serbian with a résumé in English.

202 Glotz, Gustav. "Beiträge zur Quellenkritik der Alexander-Historiker," *Jahresbericht des Königlichen Gymnasiums zu Allenstein über das Schuljahr 1893/94*, 1894, I-XIV. Greek quotations and comparisons of texts of various classical sources.

203 Goodenough, Erwin R. "The Political Philosophy of Hellenistic Kingship," *Yale Classical Studies*, I (1928), 55-102. Quotations from classical authors (translated into English), some very lengthy; also one drawing.

204 Goukowsky, P. "Le Portrait d'Alexandre," *Revue des Études Grecques*," LXXIX (1966), 495-98. Sources in the text in addition to one note.

205 Graindor, Paul. "Égypte Pharaonique. Alexandrie," *Chronique d'Egypte*, X (1935), 276-81. Text of a lecture delivered at the Egyptian University at Cairo.

206 Granier, Friedrich. "Die Makedonische Heersversammlung; ein Beitrag zum Antiken Staatsrecht," *Münchener Beiträge zur Papyrusforschung und Antiken Rechtsgeschichte*, XIII ((1931). A good bibliography, an index and many notes.

207 *Greece and Rome*, 2d. ser., XII, no. 2 (October, 1965). An anniversary issue devoted to articles concerning Alexander.

208 Griffith, G. T. "Alexander and Antipater in 323 B.C.," *African Classical Association. Proceedings*, VIII (1965), 12-17.

209 ———. "Alexander the Great and an Experiment in Government," *Cambridge Philological Society. Proceedings*, n.s., X
(1964), 23-39.

210 ———. "Alexander's Generalship at Gaugamela," *Journal of
Hellenic Studies*, LXVII (1947), 77-89. A detailed diagram of
the plan of battle of Gaugamela and a sketch of a late phase
of the battle.

211 ———. "The Letter of Darius at Arrian 2.14," *Cambridge
Philological Society. Proceedings*, CXCIV (1968), 33-48.
A list of the variant versions of peace proposals of Darius.

212 ———. "Macedonian Background," *Greece and Rome*, 2d. ser.,
XII (1965), 125-39. A discussion of the differing types of
resources available to Alexander at his accession.

213 ———. "Makedonika: Notes on the Macedonians of Philip and
Alexander," *Cambridge Philological Society. Proceedings*,
n.s., IV (1956-57), 3-10.

214 ———. "A Note on the Hipparchies of Alexander," *Journal
of Hellenic Studies*, LXXXIII (1963), 68-74.

215 Grilli, Alberto. "Plutarco, Panezio e il giudizio su Aless. Magno,"
Acme, 1952, pp. 451-57.

216 Gummerus, Herman. "Alexander den Store och Hans Rike,"
Finska Vetenskaps-Societeten, Helsingfors. Arsbok-Vuosikirja,
XX(8) (1942), 1-18. No notes; sources are mentioned in the text.

217 Gutschmid, Alfred von. "Trogus und Timagenes," *Rheinisches
Museum für Philologie*, XXXVII (1882), 548-55.

218 Haarhoff, T. J. "Alexander's Dream: The Unity of Mankind,"
Contemporary Review, CLXII (July, 1942), 48-50. An
undocumented article.

219 Habicht, Christian. "Die Herrschende Gesellschaft in den
Hellenistischen Monarchien," *Vierteljahrschrift für Sozial—
und Wirtschaftsgeschichte*, XLV (1958), 1-16.

220 Hagen, Benno von. "Isokrates und Alexander," *Philologus*,
LXVII (1908), 113-33.

221 Hamilton, J. R. "Alexander and His 'So-Called' Father," *Classical Quarterly*, n.s., III (1953), 151-57.

222 ————. "Alexander's Early Life," *Greece and Rome*, 2d. ser., XII (1965), 117-24.

223 ————. "The Cavalry Battle on the Hydaspes," *Journal of Hellenic Studies*, LXXVI (1956), 26-31.

224 ————. "Cleitarchus und Aristobulus," *Historia*, X (1961), 448-58. A discussion concerning the question of the date of Cleitarchus' writing.

225 ————. "The Letters in Plutarch's Alexander," *African Classical Association. Proceedings*, IV (1961), 9-20. Quotations in Greek drawn from Plutarch's biography of Alexander.

226 ————. "Three Passages in Arrian; Melamnidas, Menoetas, and Menidas," *Classical Quarterly*, n.s., V (1955), 217-21.

227 Hampl, Franz. "Alexander der Grosse und die Beurteilung Geschichtlicher Persönlichkeiten in der Modernen Historiographie," *La Nouvelle Clio*, VI (1954), 91-136.

228 ————. "Alexanders des Grossen Hypomnemata und Letzte Plane," *Studies Presented to D. M. Robinson* (St. Louis, Mo.: Washington University Publications, 1953), II, 816-29.

229 Hansen, Günther Christian. "Alexander und die Brahmanen," *Klio; Beiträge zur Alten Geschichte*, XLIII-XLV (1965), 351-80. Quotations in Greek from ancient sources.

230 Hartwig, P. "Ein Thongefaess des C. Popilius Mit Scenen der Alexanderschlacht," *Deutsches Archäologisches Institut. Römische Abteilung*, XIII (1898), 399-408. Illustrated.

231 Hansen, R. "Ueber die Echtheit der Briefe Alexander des Grossen," *Philologus*, XXXIX (1880), 258-304. No footnotes, but sources are cited in the text; also quotations from and comparisons of various classical sources.

232 Haupt, Herman. "Über die Altslavische übersetung des Joannes Malalas," *Hermes; Zeitschrift für Klassische Philologie*, XV

(1880), 230-35. Extensive quotations from ancient sources in Greek.

233 Haussoullier, B. "Un Rescrit d'Alexandre le Grand," *Revue de Philologie*, 1893, 188-90. The text of an inscription in Greek and a discussion of it line by line. There are no footnotes, but sources are mentioned in the text.

234 Head, Barclay V. "Coinage of Alexander the Great. An Explanation," *Numismatic Chronicle and Journal of the Royal Numismatic Society*, 3d. ser., III (1883), 18-19. Undocumented.

235 Healy, J. F. "Alexander the Great and the Last Issue of Electrum Hektai at Mytilene," *Numismatic Chronicle and Journal of the Royal Numismatic Society*, 7th. ser., II (1962), 65-71. Many illustrations.

236 Heichelheim, Fritz. "Strukturprobleme des Alexanderreiches und des Reiches der Ersten Kalifen," *Chronique d'Egypte*, VII (1932), 172-82. The text of a speech with only one note.

237 Herrmann, Léon. "La Date de l'Histoire d'Alexandre le Grande par Quinte-Curce," *Revue des Études Anciennes*, XXXI (1929), 217-24.

238 Herter, H. "Hellenismus und Hellenentum," *Das Neue Bild der Antike*, I (1942), 334-53.

239 Herzfeld, Ernst. "Der Thron des Khosro. Quellenkritische und Ikonographische Studien über Grenzgebiete der Kunstgeschichte des Morgen- und Abendlandes," *Preussische Kunstsammlungen*, Berlin. *Jahrbuch*, XLI (1920), 103-47. Illustrated.

240 Herzog, Rudolf. "Der Traum des Herondas," *Philologus*, LXXIX (1924), 370-433. Texts of fragments in Greek.

241 Heuss, Alfred. "Alexander der Grosse und die Politische Ideologie des Altertums," *Antike und Abendland*; *Beiträge zum Verständnis der Griechen und Römer und Ihres Nachlebens*, IV (1954), 65-104.

242 ———. "Antigonos Monophthalmos und die Griechischen Städte," *Hermes*; *Zeitschrift für Klassische Philologie*, LXXIII (1938), 133-94. Many quotations from classical sources.

243 ———. "Stadt und Herrscher des Hellenismus," *Klio; Beiträge zur Alten Geschichte. Beiheft*, XXXIX (1937), 1-295. An index of names, a subject index, a list of passages from ancient sources and their locations in the text, an index of page citations listed by periodical, and a list of abbreviations.

*244 Heuzey, Leon. "La Nécropole Royale de Sidon," *République Française*, May 17, 1892. Only location in the United States is at Harvard University. Their file is incomplete and does not include this issue.

245 Heydemann, Heinrich. "Alexander der Grosse und Darios Kodomannos auf Unteritalischen Vasenbildern," *Archäologische Gesellschaft zu Berlin. Winckelmannsprogramm der Archäologischen Gesellschaft zu Berlin*, VIII (1883), 1-26. Illustrations, one fold-out.

246 Highet, Gilbert. "Great Confrontations: Diogenes and Alexander," *Horizon*, V (Mar., 1963), 10-13. One color plate but no notes.

247 Hill, G. F. "Alexander the Great and the Persian Lion-Gryphon," *Journal of Hellenic Studies*, XLIII (1923), 156-61. Plates of gold staters.

248 ———. "Notes on the Alexandrine Coinage of Phoenicia," *Numisma*, IV (1909), 1-15. Contains a chronology of Alexandrine coins of Phoenicia.

249 Hogarth, D. G. "Alexander in Egypt and Some Consequences," *Journal of Egyptian Archaeology*, II (1915), 53-60. A lecture given before the Egypt Exploration Fund on December 8, 1914; no footnotes.

250 ———. "The Army of Alexander," *Journal of Philology*, XVII (1888), 1-26.

251 ———. "The Deification of Alexander the Great," *English Historical Review*, II (1887), 317-29.

252 Ideler, Herrn. "Ueber das Todesjahr Alexanders des Grossen," *Akademie der Wissenschaften, Berlin. Historisch-Philologischen Klasse. Abhandlungen*, 1820/21, pp. 261-88. Quotations in Greek from ancient sources.

253 Instinsky, Hans Ulrich. "Alexander, Pindar, Euripides," *Historia*, X (1961), 248-55. A quotation in Greek from Euripides.

254 Jacoby, Carl. "Ktesias und Diodor, eine Quellenuntersuchung von Diodor B. II, c. 1-34," *Rheinisches Museum für Philologie*, XXX (1875), 555-615. Comparisons of the texts of Diodorus, Curtius and Strabo, and of Diodorus and Curtius.

255 Jacoby, F. "Die Alexandergeschichte des Anaximenes," *Hermes*; *Zeitschrift für Klassische Philologie*, LVIII (1923), 457-58.

256 ———. "Die Beisetzungen Alexanders des Grossen," *Rheinisches Museum für Philologie*, LVIII (1903), 461-62.

257 ———. "Ueber Das Marmor Parium," *Rheinisches Museum für Philologie*, LIX (1904), 63-107. The full text of the fragments in Greek and a comparison of them line by line.

258 Jäger, Oscar. "Alexander der Grosse als Regent," *Preussische Jahrbücher*, LXX (1892), 68-105. Printed in the old German type.

259 ———. "Bemerkungen zur Geschichte Alexanders des Grossen," *Programm des Koniglichen Gymnasiums zu Wetzlar, für das Schuljahr von Michaelis 1860 bis Michaelis 1861* (Wetzlar, 1861), pp. 3-12. Printed in the old German type.

260 Jaeger, Werner. "Aristotle's Politics," *Hibbert Journal; a Quarterly Review of Religion, Theology, and Philosophy*, XXV (Jan., 1927), 335-46. An undocumented article translated into English by Professor J. L. Stocks.

261 Janke, A. "Die Schlacht bei Issos," *Klio; Beiträge zur Alten Geschichte*, X (1910), 137-77. Photographs of the site and maps showing elevations.

262 Jeep, Justus. "Kritische Bemerkungen zu Q. Curtius Rufus," *Neue Jahrbücher für Philologie und Paedagogik*, XCI (1865), 189-96.

263 Jones, Tom B. "Alexander and the Winter of 330-329 B.C.," *Classical Weekly*, XXVIII (Feb., 1935), 124-25.

264 Jordanus, J. "Inest Commentatio in Plutarchi Vitae Alexandri Capita Aliquot, Enarrandi in Scholis Eiusdem Scriptoris Specimen

Tertium," *Sollennia Anniversaria in Gymnasio Regio Onoldino die XXVIII. Mensis Augusti Celebranda* (Typis Brügelianis, 1848), 1-23.

265 Jouguet, Pierre. "Alexandre à l'Oasis d'Ammon et le Témoignage de Callisthène," *Institut d'Egypte, Cairo. Bulletin,* 6th. ser., XXVI, (1944), 91-107. Quotations in Greek and Latin.

266 ———. "La Date Alexandrine de la Fondation d'Alexandrie," *Revue des Études Anciennes,* XLII (1940), 192-97.

267 ———. "Trois Etudes sur l'Hellénisme: L'Empire d'Alexandre, L'État Égyptien Ptolemaïque, Le Rôle d' Alexandrie," *Université Farouk. Faculté des Lettres. Publications,* I (1944), 1-47. An index and a bibliography for the last essay.

268 Judeich, Walther. "Alexander der Grosse und der Hellenismus," *Antike Schlachtfelder,* IV (1924/31), 345-446. A brief bibliography at the beginning of each section and a list of soldiers by place.

269 ———. "Der Grabherr des 'Alexandersarkophags'," *Deutsches Archäologisches Institut. Jahrbuch,* X (1895), 165-82. Illustrations (details of the sarcophagus).

270 ———. "Die Schlacht am Granikos," *Klio; Beiträge zur Alten Geschichte,* VIII (1908), 372-97. Many photographs, maps, and a battle plan.

271 Junge, P. J. "Hazarapatiš. Zur Stellung des Chiliarchen der Klg. Leibgarde im Achämenidenstaat," *Klio; Beiträge zur Alten Geschichte,* XXXIII (1940), 13-38.

272 Jurien de la Gravière. "Les Deux Dernières Campagnes d'Alexandre," *Revue des Deux Mondes,* 9th. ser., IV (July, 1882), 62-105. Only 3 notes, but additional sources are noted in the text.

273 Kaerst, J. "Alexander der Grosse und der Hellenismus," *Historische Zeitschrift,* LXXIV (1895), 1-43, 193-230. Printed in the old German type.

274 ———. "Die Begründung des Alexander—und Ptolemaeerkultes in Aegypten," *Rheinisches Museum für Philologie,* LII (1897), 42-68.

275 ———. "Der Briefwechsel Alexanders d. Gr.," *Philologus*, LVI (1897), 406-12; also in n.f., V (1892), 602-22. Few footnotes but additional sources are given in text; also a comparison of Plutarch and Arrian.

276 ———. "Der Korinthische Bund," *Rheinisches Museum für Philologie*, n.f., LII (1897), 519-56. Greek quotations.

277 ———. "Ptolemaios und die Ephemeriden Alexanders d. Gr.," *Philologus*, LVI (1897) 334-39.

278 ———. "Untersuchungen über Timagenes von Alexandreia," *Philologus*, LVI (1897), 621-57. A comparison of the texts of Justin and Strabo, and of Curtius and Justin.

279 Kahrstedt, Ulrich. "Das Athenische Köntingent zum Alexanderzuge," *Hermes*; *Zeitschrift für Klassische Philologie*, LXXI (1936), 120-24.

280 Kallenberg, Hermann. "Die Quellen für die Nachrichten der Alten Historiker über die Diadochenkämpfe bis zum tode des Eumenes und der Olympias," *Philologus*, XXXVI (1875), 305-27, 488-528, 637-70; XXXVII (1876), 193-227. Comparisons of texts (some long) of Arrian, Diodorus, Justin, Dexippus, Curtius, Plutarch, and Nepos.

*281 Kanatsoule, Demetrios. "Miá Poreiá toû M. 'Alexandrou," *Makedonikon Hemerologion*, 1950, pp. 81-88. Only copy of this title in the United States is at the Library of Congress and they do not have this volume.

282 Kanatsulis, D. "Antipatros als Feldherr und Staatsmann in der Zeit Philipps und Alexanders des Grossen," *Hellenica*; *Philologikon, Historikon kai Laographikon Periodikon Syngramma*, XVI (1958/9), 14-64.

283 Keil, Josef. "Der Kampf um den Granikosübergang und das Strategische Problem der Issosschlacht," *Verein Klassischer Philologen. Mitteilungen*, I (1924), 13-19.

284 ———. "Persönlichkeiten aus der Werdezeit des Hellenismus," *Akademie der Wissenschaften, Vienna. Philosophisch-Historische*

Klasse. Anzeiger, LXXXVII (1950), 1-4. No notes; a bibliography at the end.

285 Kekule von Stradonitz, Reinhard. "Über das Bruchstück einer Portraitstatuette Alexander's des Grossen," *Akademie der Wissenschaften, Berlin. Sitzungsberichte,* 1899, pp. 280-88. Illustrations.

286 Kern, Edward. "The Godlike Conqueror," *Life,* LIV (May 3, 1963), 63-65. Many plates; no footnotes.

287 Kern, O. "Der Glaube Alexanders des Grossen," *Forschungen und Fortschritte; Korrespondenzblatt der Deutschen Wissenschaft und Technik,* XXXV-XXXVI (1938), 405-07. Undocumented.

288 Kienast, Dietmar. "Alexander und der Ganges," *Historia,* XIV (1965), 180-88. Quotes in Greek from Arrian and Diodorus.

289 Kleiner, Gerhard. "Alexanders Reichsmünzen," *Deutschen Akademie der Wissenschaften, Berlin. Abhandlungen,* 1947 (Nr. 5). A chronological table and one plate.

290 ———. "Das Bildnis Alexanders des Grossen," *Deutsches Archäologisches Institut. Jahrbuch,* LXV-LXVI (1950-51), 206-30. Some illustrations.

291 Klučka, M. "Několik Poznámek o Pojetí Alexandra vel. v Díle Pedagoga J. A. Komenského," *Listy Filologicke,* V (1957), 90-97. No footnotes; sources are mentioned in the text.

292 Knapowski, Roch. "Finanse Wojenne Aleksandra Wielkiego," *Poznanskie Towarzystow Przyjaciol Nauk, Posen. Sprawozdania,* XIII (1946), 41-42. No footnotes; sources are cited in the text.

293 Koch, Herbert. "Zum 'Alexander Mit der Lanze,' " in *Neue Beiträge zur Klassischen Altertumswissenschaft. Festschrift zum 60. Geburtstag von Bernhard Schweitzer,* ed. by Reinhard Lullies (Stuttgart: W. Kohlhammer, [1954]), pp. 240-42.

294 Köhler, Arthur. "Reichsverwaltung und Politik Alexanders des Grossen," *Klio; Beiträge zur Alten Geschichte,* V (1905), 303-16.

295 Köhler, Ulrich. "Über die Diadochengeschichte Arrian's," *Akademie der Wissenschaften, Berlin. Sitzungsberichte*, 1890, pp. 557-88. Quotations in Greek from ancient sources.

296 ———. "Die Eroberung Asiens durch Alexander den Grossen und der Korinthische Bund," *Preussischen Akademie der Wissenschaften, Berlin. Sitzungsberichte*, 1898, pp. 120-34 Many quotations from ancient sources.

297 ———. "Aus der Finanzverwaltung Lykurgs," *Hermes: Zeitschrift für Klassische Philologie*, V (1871), 223-27. Reproductions of inscriptions and many quotations in Greek from ancient sources.

298 ———. "Studien zu den Attischen Psephismen," *Hermes; Zeitschrift für Klassische Philologie*, V (1871), 1-20. Contains reproductions of inscriptions and extensive quotations in Greek from ancient sources.

299 ———. "Über das Verhältniss Alexander's des Grossen zu Seinem Vater Philipp," *Akademie der Wissenschaften, Berlin. Sitzungsberichte*, 1892, pp. 497-514.

300 Koepp, Friedrich. "Alexander der Grosse," *Monographien zur Weltgeschichte*, IX (1899), 1-96. A large map, 85 pictures, an index, and sources listed in the text (no notes given).

301 ———. "Aristoteles und Alexander," *Sonderabdruck aus den Preussischen Jahrbüchern*, CXIII (1903), heft 1, 83-100. Quotations from ancient sources. Printed in the old German type.

302 ———. "Über das Bibdnis Alexanders des Grossen," *Archäologische Gesellschaft zu Berlin. Winckelmannsprogramm der Archäologischen Gesellschaft zu Berlin* (Berlin: Georg Reimer, 1892). Many illustrations in addition to its many notes.

303 Körte, A. "Anaximenes von Lampsakos als Alexanderhistoriker," *Rheinisches Museum für Philologie*, LXI (1906), 476-80.

304 Körte, G. "Das Alexander-Mosaik aus Pompeji," *Deutsches Archäologisches Institut. Römische Abteilung*, XXII (1907), 1-24.

305 Kolbe, Walther. "Die Weltreichsidee Alexanders des Grossen," *Freiburger Wissenschaftliche Gesellschaft*, XXV (1936).

306 Kolster, W. H. "Alexander der Grosse," *Sammlung Gemeinver-standlicher Wissenschaftlicher Vortrage*, V (1890), no. 99, 1-39. An undocumented article printed in the old German type.

307 Kornemann, Ernst. "Alexander der Grosse und die Makedonen in Ptolemaios' I. Alexandergeschichte, Staaten, Völker, Männer," *Das Erbe der Alten; Schriften über Wesen und Wirkung der Antike*, n.s., XXIV (1934), 52-77.

308 ———. "Zur Geschichte der Antiken Herscherkulte," *Klio*; *Beiträge zur Alten Geschichte*, I (1902), 51-146. One table.

309 ———. "Zur Geschichte der Gracchenzeit; Quellenkritische und Chronologische Untersuchungen," *Klio*; *Beiträge zur Alten Geschichte*, I (1894), 1-56. A comparison of the texts of Orosius, Plutarch and Appian; also a table comparing several classical authors on various subjects.

310 ———. "Die Letzten Ziele der Politik Alexanders des Grossen," *Klio*; *Beiträge zur Alten Geschichte*, XVI (1920), 209-33.

311 ———. "Zur Politik der Ersten Nachfolger Alexanders des Grossen," *Vergangenheit und Gegenwart*, XVI (1926), 333-45. Printed in the old German type, with quotations in Greek from ancient sources.

312 Kovalev, S. I. "Aleksandr i Klit" (Alexander and Kleitos), *Akademiia Nauk S.S.S.R. Institut Istorii. Vestnik Drevnei Istorii*, III (1949), no. 20, 69-73. Written in Russian.

313 ———. "Monarkhiya Aleksandra Makedonskovo" (The Monarchy of Alexander the Great), *Akademiia Nauk, S.S.S.R. Institut Istorii. Vestnik Drevnei Istorii*, IV (1949), no. 30, 29-40. An undocumented article, written in Russian.

314 Krause, A. "Beiträge zur Alexander-Greschichte," Hermes; *Zeitschrift für Klassische Philologie*, XXV (1890), 62-81.

315 ———. "Miscellen zur Geschichte Alexanders," *Hermes*; *Zeitschrift für Klassische Philologie*, XXIII (1888), 525-31.

316 Kromayers, J. "Alexander der Grosse und die Hellenistische Entwicklung in dem Jahrhundert nach seinem Tode," *Historische Zeitschrift*, C (1908), 11-52.

317 Krumbholz, Paul. "Diodors Assyrische Geschichte," *Rheinisches Museum für Philologie*, XLI (1886), 321-41. Long quotations in Greek from ancient sources and a comparison of the texts of Diodorus and Athenaeus.

318 Lamer, Hans. "Alexanders Zug in die Oase Siwa," *Klio; Beiträge zur Alten Geschichte*, XXIV (1931), 63-69.

319 Lammert, E. "Janke, A. Auf Alexanders des Grossen Pfaden. Eine Reise durch Kleinasien. Berlin: Weidmann, 1904," *Berliner Philologische Wochenschrift*, 1905, col. 999-1010 and 1063-71. A detailed, annotated discussion of Janke's book.

320 Lamotte, É. "Les Premières Relations entre l'Inde et l'Occident," *La Nouvelle Clio*, V (1953), 83-118.

321 Laqueur, Richard. "Hellenismus," *Giessen. Universität. Schriften der Hessischen Hochschulen*, I (1924), 1-36.

322 Larsen, Jakob A. O. "An Additional Note on Alexander at the Oracle of Ammon," *Classical Philology*, XXVII (1932), 274-75. Undocumented.

323 ———. "Alexander at the Oracle of Ammon," *Classical Philology*, XXVII (1932), 70-75. Only one footnote but many sources are cited in the text.

324 Lauth, F. J. "Alexander in Aegypten," *Akademie der Wissenschaften, Munich. Historische-Classe. Abhandlungen*, XIV (1876) 97-164.

325 Leclant, Jean. " 'Per Africae Sitientia.' Témoignages des Sources Classiques sur les Pistes Menant à l'Oasis d'Ammon," *Cairo. Institut Français d'Archeologie Orientale. Bulletin*, XLIX (1950), 193-253. A discussion of ancient sources with texts of fragments and inscriptions in Greek.

326 Lederer, Philip. "Ein Beitrag zum Münzbildnis Alexanders des Grossen," *Revue Suisse de Numismatique*, XXVIII (1941), 7-23. Illustrations; notes collected at the end.

327 ———. "Ein Goldstater Alexanders des Grossen," *Zeitschrift für Numismatik*, XXXIII (1922), 185-205. Two views of the coin in question.

328 Lehmann, C. F. "Zu den Ephemeriden Alexanders des Grossen," *Hermes*; *Zeitschrift für Klassische Philologie*, XXXVI (1901), 319-20.

329 Lehmann, Konrad. "Die Schlacht am Granikos," *Klio*; *Beiträge zur Alten Geschichte*, XI (1911), 230-44. Quotations in Greek from ancient sources.

330 Lehmann-Haupt, C. F. "Zu Alexanders Zug in die Oase Siwa," *Klio*; *Beiträge zur Alten Geschichte*, XXIV (1931), 169-90. Many quotations in Greek from ancient sources.

331 ———. "Nachträgliches zu Alexanders Zug in die Oase Siwa," *Klio*; *Beiträge zur Alten Geschichte*, XXIV (1931), 376-80.

332 Lenormant, François. "Note sur Deux Ateliers Monétaires d'Alexandre le Grand," *Revue Numismatique*, 1863, pp. 169-75. Quotations in Greek from ancient sources.

333 Lenschau, Thomas. "Alexander der Grosse und Chios," *Klio*; *Beiträge zur Alten Geschichte*, XXXIII (1940), 201-24. The text of an inscription in Greek.

334 "A Lesson from Alexander," *Century Magazine*, LVII (1898/99), 796. An undocumented editorial.

335 Lévi, Sylvain. "Notes sur l'Inde à l'Epoque d'Alexandre," *Journal Asiatique*; *Recueil de Memoires et de Notices Relatifs aux Études Orientales*, XV (1890), 234-40.

336 Lippold, Georg. "Zum Alexandersarkophag," *Archaiologikè Ephēmeris*. *Archaiologikē Hetairia en Athēnais*, XCII–XCIII (1953-54), 214-20. Illustrated.

337 Lorentz, Friedrich von. "Eine Bronzestatuette Alexanders des Grossen," *Deutsches Archäologisches Institut*. *Römische Abteilung*. *Mitteilungen*, I (1935), 333-38. An abstract appears in English in the *American Journal of Archaeology*, XLI (1937), 126-27.

338 Luedecke, Maximilianus. "De Fontibus Quibus Usus Arrianus Anabasin Composuit," *Leipziger Studien zur Classischen Philologie*, XI (1889), 3-86. An index of the *Anabasis*, an index by subject, many Greek quotations, and the following comparisons: Curtius and Arrian; Strabo and Arrian; Appian and Strabo; Plutarch and

Strabo; Arrian, Plutarch, and Strabo; the *Anabasis* and the *Indica*; Arrian and Plutarch.

339　Luschnat, Otto. "Diem Perditi," *Philologus*, CIX (1965), 297-99.

340　McCrindle, J. W. "The Campaigns of Alexander the Great in Turkistan," *Scottish Geographical Magazine*, X (Nov., 1894), 590-95.

341　MacMunn, George. "The Rock of Aornos," *Nineteenth Century and After*, C (1926), 449-54. No notes although ancient sources are mentioned in the text.

342　Macurdy, Grace H. "The Refusal of Callisthenes to Drink the Health of Alexander," *Journal of Hellenic Studies*, L (1930), 294-97.

343　————. "Roxane and Alexander IV in Epirus," *Journal of Hellenic Studies*, LII (1932), 256-61.

344　Malden, H. E. "Alexander in Afghanistan," *Journal of Philology*, XII (1883), 271-77. Few footnotes, but ancient sources are mentioned in the text.

345　Mallet, M. Dominique. "Les Rapports des Grecs avec l'Egypte (de la Conquête de Cambyse, 525, a celle d'Alexandre, 331)," *Cairo. Institut. Français d'Archaeologie Orientale. Memoires*, XLVIII (1922), 1-219. A table of contents, an index, Greek quotations and Hieroglyphic quotations; various appendices.

346　Mamroth, Alfred. "Einiges über die Porträtierungen der Nachfolger Alexander des Grossen," *Berliner Numismatische Zeitschrift*, 1951, pp. 185-89.

347　Marquart, J. "Alexanders Marsch von Persepolis nach Heràt," *Philologus. Supplementband*, X (1907), 19-71. Part of a larger article which contains many notes, tables, comparisons of the texts of Arrian, Diodorus and Curtius in German, and of Curtius and Budge; also a subject and name index, a Greek word index, and one for various languages of the area.

348　Mathieu, Georges. "Deux Manuscrits Méconnus de la Rhetorique à Alexandre," *Revue de Philologie*, n. s., XLVII (1923), 58-64.

349 ————. "Notes sur Athènes à la Veille de la Guerre Lamiaque," *Revue de Philologie,* LV (1929), 159-83. Many Greek quotations and a comparative table of relative populations by date.

350 deMauriac, Henry M. "Alexander the Great and the Politics of 'Homonoia,' " *Journal of the History of Ideas,* X (1949), 104-14.

351 May, J. M. F. "The Alexander Coinage of Nikokles of Paphos, with a Note on Some Recently Identified Tetradrachms from the Demanhur Find," *Numismatic Chronicle and Journal of the Royal Numismatic Society,* 6th. ser., XII (1952), 1-18. A list of coins by group with word descriptions, then by place and mint; also a plate.

352 Méautis, Georges. "La Psychologie d'Alexandre le Grand dans le Littérature Latine," *Mélanges Offerts à Max Niedermann à l'Occasion de Son Soixante-Dixieme Anniversaire* (Neuchâtel: Université. Faculté des Lettres. Recueil de Travaux, Fasc. 22, 1944), pp. 115-18.

353 ————. "Research sur l'Époque d'Alexandre," *Revue des Études Ancienne,* XLIV (1942), 300-08.

354 Meinecke, Friedrich. "Johann Gustav Droysen; sein Briefwechsel und seine Geschichtsschreibung," *Historische Zeitschrift,* CXLI (1929), 249-87. A biography of Droysen and a discussion of his works.

355 Mensching, Eckart. "Peripatetiker über Alexander," *Historia,* XII (1963), 274-82.

356 Merlan, Philip. "Alexander the Great or Antiphon the Sophist?," *Classical Philology,* XLV (1950), 161-66. Quotations of a section of Plutarch and of an Antiphon fragment (both in Greek).

357 ————. "Isocrates, Aristotle, and Alexander the Great," *Historia,* III (1954), 60-81. A discussion concerning the letters of Isocrates to Alexander.

358 Messina, G. "Tramonto ed Aurora di Civiltà," *Civiltà Cattolica,* CVI(2) (1955), 275-83.

359 Meyer, Eduard. "Alexander der Grosse und die Absolute Monarchie," *Kleine Schriften,* I (1924), 267-314.

360 ————. "Alexander the Great and Universal Monarchy,"
International Quarterly, VIII (1903), 280-95. Translated into
English by C. B. Stetson.

361 ————. "Arrians Geschichte Alexanders des Grossen," *Hermes*;
Zeitschrift für Klassische Philologie, XXXIII (1898), 648-52.

362 ————. "Die Makedonischen Militärcolonien," *Hermes*;
Zeitschrift für Klassische Philologie, XXXIII (1898), 643-47.
Quotations from ancient sources.

363 Meyer, Ernst. "Alexander und der Ganges," *Klio*; *Beiträge zur
Alten Geschichte*, XXI (1926), 183-91. Many quotations from
ancient sources.

364 Michalaros, Demetrios A. "Macedonia and the World," *Athene*,
XXII(1) (1961), 3-13, 70. A map, many photos of famous
Macedonian statesmen, and a list of Macedonian rulers from
Alexander to the Roman occupation (168 B.C.). A brief history
to the present.

365 Michon, Étienne. "L'Hermès d'Alexandre Dit Hermès Azara,"
Revue Archéologique, I (6th. ser., vol. VII) (1906), 79-110.

366 Miller, Anton. "Die Alexandergeschichte nach Strabo," *Festgabe
an die Ehrwürdige Julia Maximilianea zu Würzburg zu Ihrer Dritten
Säkularfeier, Pietätsvoll Gewidmet von dem Lehrerkollegium
der K. Studienanstalt Würzburg*, 1882, pp. 1-66. Margin notes,
quotations in Greek from ancient sources and diagrams, but no
footnotes.

367 ————. "Die Alexandergeschichte nach Strabo," *Festgabe des
Lehrerkollegiums des K. Alten Gymnasiums zu Würzburg*, 1891,
pp. 1-25. A table of contents, quotations in Greek from ancient
sources, comparisons of various authors with Arrian, and a name
index.

*368 Milne, J. G. "Alexander at the Oasis of Ammon," *Miscellanea
Gregoriana*, 1941, pp. 145-49. The title is listed in the *Bulletin
of the Institute Française d'Archeologie Orientale*, vol. XLIX.

369 Milns, R. D. "Alexander's Macedonian Cavalry and Diodorus
XVII 17.4," *Journal of Hellenic Studies*, LXXXVI (1966), 167-8.

370 ———. "Alexander's Pursuit of Darius Through Iran," *Historia*, XV (1966), 256. No footnotes; sources are cited in the text.

371 ———. "Alexander's Seventh Phalanx Battalion," *Greek, Roman and Byzantine Studies*, VII (2) (1966), 159-66. A list of Macedonian infantry and garrison troop losses by battle.

372 ———. "Curtius Rufus and the 'Historiae Alexandri,' " *Latomus*, XXV (1966), 490-507.

373 Miltner, Franz. "Alexanders Strategie bei Issos," *Oesterreichisches Archäologisches Institut. Jahreshefte*, XXVIII (1933), 69-78 A map.

374 ———. "Die Staatsrechtliche Entwiklung des Alexanderreiches," *Klio; Beiträge zur Alten Geschichte*, XXVI (1933), 39-55.

375 Mitchel, Fordyce. "Athens in the Age of Alexander," *Greece and Rome*, 2d. ser., XII (1965), 189-204.

376 Modī, Jīvanjī Jamshedjī. "Alexander the Great and the Destruction of the Ancient Literature of the Parsees at His Hands," *Oriental Conference Papers; Papers Read at the Oriental Conferences Held in India* (Bombay: The Fort Printing Press, 1932), pp. 58-116. Paper read at the Second Oriental Conference in 1922. Contains margin notes as well as quotations in Arabic.

377 Momigliano, Arnaldo. "Re e Popolo in Macedonia Prima di Alessandro Magno," *Athenaeum*, XIII (1935), 3-21. Few footnotes; additional sources are cited in the text.

378 Morel, W. "Zur Späteren Griechischen Prosa," *Hermes; Zeitschrift für Klassische Philologie*, LXV (1930), 367-68. No footnotes, sources are cited in the text.

379 Muller, F. "De Epistula Alexandri ad Artistotelem Observatiunculae," *Mnemosyne. Bibliotheca Philologica Batava*, n.s., LIII (1925), 268-72.

380 Mussche, Herman Frank. "Recherches sur la Sculpture Gréco-Romaine au Liban et en Syrie Occidentale d'Alexandre le Grand à Constantin," *Congrès International d'Archéologie. 7th. Atti*, I (1958), 437-42. Various tables.

381 Narain, A. K. "Alexander and India," *Greece and Rome,* 2d. ser., XII (1965), 155-65.

382 Naue, Julius. "Die Porträitdarstellung Alexanders des Grossen auf Griechischen Münzen des Königs Lysimachus von Thracien," *Zeitschrift für Numismatik,* VIII (1881), 29-53. A list of statues and their present locations, descriptions of coins, and many illustrations.

383 Neppi Modona, Aldo. "Chi Fu Il Primo Vero 'Reggente' Dopo la Morte di Alessandro Magno?," *Athenaeum; Studii Periodici di Letteratura e Storia,* X (1932), 22-36. Quotations in Greek from ancient sources.

384 Neubert, Max. "Alexanders des Grossen Balkanzug," *Petermanns Geographische Mitteilungen,* LXXX (1934), 281-89.

385 Neumann, Karl Johannes. "Die Fahrt des Patrokles auf dem Kaspischen Meere und der Alte Lauf des Oxos," *Hermes; Zeitschrift für Klassische Philologie,* XIX (1884), 165-85.

386 ———. "Zur Landeskunde und Geischichte Kilikiens, mit Beiträgen zur Kritik der Geschichtschreiber Alexanders," *Neue Jahrbücher für Phililogie und Paedagogik,* CXXVII (1883), 527-51.

387 Newell, Edward T. "Alexander Hoards I. Introduction and Kyparissa," *Numismatic Notes and Monographs,* IIII (1921), 1-21. A list of the coins in the hoard and plates of some of the coins.

388 ———. "Alexander Hoards II: Demanhur," *Numismatic Notes and Monographs,* XIX (1923), 1-162. A catalog of the varieties of coins in the hoard and plates of some; also a discussion of the various uses to which coins may be put in historical research.

389 ———. "Alexander Hoards III. Andritsaena," *Numismatic Notes and Monographs,* XXI (1923), 1-39. A list of coins in the hoard and many plates.

390 ———. "Alexander Hoards IV. Olympia," *Numismatic Notes and Monographs,* XXXIX (1929). A short discussion of coins which contains many plates, notes, and a discussion of mints.

391 ———. "The Alexandrine Coinage of Sinope," *American Journal of Numismatics*, LII (1918), 117-27.

392 ———. "The Dated Alexander Coinage of Sidon and Ake," *Yale Oriental Series. Researches*, II (1916). A list of coins by series and group with word descriptions for each area, a list of coin collections, a discussion of each series, and plates and an index for the plates.

393 ———. "Myriandros-Alexandria Kat'Isson," *American Journal of Numismatics*, LIII (1919), pt. 2, 1-42. A list of coins and "Alexandrine Issues."

394 ———. "Nikokles, King of Paphos," *Numismatic Chronicle and Journal of the Royal Numismatic Society*, 4th ser., XIX (1919), 64-65. An undocumented correction to his "Some Cypriote Alexanders."

395 ———. "Reattribution of Certain Tetradrachms of Alexander the Great," *American Journal of Numismatics*, XLV (1911), 1-10, 37-45, 113-25, 194-200; XLVI (1912), 22-24, 37-49, 109-16. A catalog of coins with Müller's numbers and a word description; plates.

396 ———. "Some Cypriote 'Alexanders,' " *Numismatic Chronicle and Journal of the Royal Numismatic Society*, 4th ser., XV (1915), 294-322. Several plates.

397 ———. "Tarsos under Alexander," *American Journal of Numismatics*, LII (1918), 69-115. A list of coins.

398 Newman, F. W. "Moral Estimate of Alexander the Great," *Littell's Living Age*, CXXXIV (1875), 3-17. The same article appeared in *Fraser's Magazine*, XCI (1875), 667-85.

399 Nicholson, Sir Harold. "The Mystery That Was Alexander," *Life*, XXXIX (Nov. 14, 1955), 86ff. A chronological table, many illustrations, a map, but no notes.

400 Niese, Benedictus. "Zur Würdingung Alexander's des Grossen," *Historische Zeitschrift*, LXXIX (1897), 1-44. Printed in the old German type.

401 Nissen, H. "Die Abfassungszeit von Arrians Anabasis," *Rheinisches Museum für Philologie*, n.f., XLIII (1888), 236-57 Quotations from classical sources.

*402 Nock, Arthur Darby. "Hellenistic Religion—the Two Phases," in *Syllabus of Gifford Lectures*, 1st. ser., 1939. The Library of Congress reports that the only United States location is the Dumbarton Oaks Research Library; they say that they do not own this title.

403 ————. "Notes on Ruler-Cult, I-IV," *Journal of Hellenic Studies*, XLVIII (1928), 21-43. Many photos of coins and their descriptions.

404 Noe, Sydney P. "The Alexander Coinage of Sicyon. Arranged from Notes of Edward T. Newell with Comments and Additions by Sydney P. Noe," *Numismatic Studies*, VI (1950). A table of contents, plates, an index of symbols, letters, and monograms, and a catalog of coins by group with word descriptions.

405 ————. "A Bibliography of Greek Coin Hoards," *Numismatic Notes and Monographs*, XXV (1925). An index by mints and rulers and a geographical index. For each hoard the following information is given: place, where discovered, type of coin, and disposition.

406 Norden, E. "Ein Panegyricus auf Augustus in Virgils Aeneis," *Rheinisches Museum für Philologie*, LIV (1899), 466-82. Quotations from ancient sources.

407 Nougayrol, Jean. "Une Ère d'Alexandre le Grand en Babylonie?," *Bibliotheca Orientalis*, IX (1952), 166-67. A documented examination of the text of an inscription.

408 Oekonomidis, Al. N. "On the Portraits of Alexander the Great Used as Models for Portraits of Mithradates the Great," *Archeion Pontou*, XXII (1958), 234-43. In Greek with an English résumé; many photographs. See also entry 411.

409 Oertel, Friedrich. "Alexander der Grosse in Neuer Sicht," *Orientalistische Literaturzeitung*, LII (1957), col. 101-08.

410 ———. "Zur Ammonsohnschaft Alexanders," *Rheinisches Museum für Philologie*, LXXXIX (1940), 66-74.

411 Oikonomides, Al. N. "Notes on Portraits of Alexander the Great," *Athene*, XXII(1) (1961), 24-31. Many photographs; no footnotes, but sources are cited in the text.

412 Ōmuta, Akira. "The 'Deification' of Alexander," *Journal of Classical Studies*, X (1962), 88-99. In Japanese with an English résumé on pp. 170-71.

413 Oppert, J. "Alexandre à Babylone," *Académie des Inscriptions et Belles-Lettres, Paris. Comptes-Rendus des Seances*, 4th. ser., XXVI (1898), 413-46. Contains quotations from Strabo and an appendix—"Les Cycles de Meton" (a listing of archons of Athens by Olympiad and year) from 433 B.C. to 255 B.C.

414 Otto, Walter. "Alexander der Grosse; Ein Kriegsvortrag," *Marburger Akademische Reden*, XXXIV (1916), 1-42. Printed in the old German type. No notes but some sources are cited in the text.

415 Pagenstecher, Rudolf. "Alexandrinische Studien," *Heidelberger Akademie der Wissenschaften. Philosophisch-Historische Klasse. Sitzungsberichte*, VIII (1917), abh. 12. A table of contents, notes, plates, and an index.

416 Paribeni, Roberto. "La Macedonia Sino ad Alessandro Magno," *Milan. Università Cattolica del Sacro Cuore. Pubblicazioni*, n.s., XVI (1947), 1-113. A table of contents, notes, and a bibliography.

417 Parthey, G. "Das Orakel und die Oase des Ammon," *Akademie der Wissenschaften, Berlin. Abhandlungen*, 1862, pp. 131-94. No notes, but sources are mentioned in the text; a table of contents at the end.

418 Pasquali, Giorgio. "Alessandro all'Oasi di Ammone e Callisthene," *Rivista di Filologia e d'Istruzione Classica*, LVII (n.s., VII) (1929), 513-21. Quotations from ancient sources.

419 ———. "Ancora Alessandro all' Oasi di Ammone e Callisthene," *Rivista di Filologia e d'Istruzione Classica*, LVIII (n.s., VIII) (1930), 342-44.

420 Pearson, C. "Alexander, Porus and the Punjab," *Indian Antiquary; a Journal of Oriental Research in Archaeology, Epigraphy, Ethnology, Geography, History, Folklore, Languages, Literature, Numismatics, Philosophy, Religion*, XXXIV (1905), 253-61. A prefatory note by Vincent A. Smith and a map.

421 Pearson, Lionel. "The Diary and Letters of Alexander the Great," *Historia*, III (1954), 429-59. A bibliographical note to explain abbreviations and list of works most often cited.

422 ———. "The Story of Alexander, as Told by His Chief Statesman, Onesicritus," *Classical Association, London. Proceedings*, XLVIII (1951), 31-32. An undocumented summary of a paper presented to the Association on Apr. 5, 1951.

423 Perdrizet, Paul. "Un Type Inédit de la Plastique Grecque: Alexandre à l'Égide," *Fondation Eugène Piot. Monuments et Mémoires*, XXI (1913), 59-72. Two plates of statues.

424 ———. "Venatio Alexandri," *Journal of Hellenic Studies*, XIX (1899), 273-79. A plate and many footnotes.

425 Pernice, Erich. "Bemerkungen zum Alexandermosaik," *Deutsches Archäologisches Institut. Römische Abteilung*, XXII (1907), 25-34.

426 ———. "Nachtraegliche Bemerkungen zum Alexandermosaik," *Deutsches Archäologisches Institut. Römische Abteilung*, XXIII (1908), 11-14.

427 Perrot, Georges. "Les Sarcophages Grecques de Sidon au Musée Impérial de Constantinople," *Journal des Débats*, April 12, 1892.

428 Petas, Photios. "New Discoveries at Pella—Birthplace and Capital of Alexander," *Archaeology*, XI (1958), 246-54. Many photos of the area but is not documented.

429 Petersen, Eugene. "Der Leichenwagen Alexanders des Grossen," *Neue Jahrbücher für Klassische Altertum, Geschichte und*

Deutsche Litteratur und für Pädagogik, XV (1905), 698-710.
Many drawings of the hearse.

430 Pfeiffer, Rudolf. "Berenikēs Plokamos," *Philologus,* LXXXVII
(1932), 179-228. The texts of fragments in Greek.

431 Pfister, Friedrich. "Alexander der Grosse. Die Geschichte Seines
Ruhms im Lichte Seiner Beinamen," *Historia,* XIII (1964), 37-79.

432 ———. "Alexander der Grosse in den Offenbarungen der
Griechen, Juden, Mohammedaner und Christen," *Akademie der
Wissenschaften, Berlin. Sektion für Altertumswissenschaft.
Schriften,* III (1956), 1-55. A table of contents.

433 ———. "Alexander der Grosse in der Bildenden Kunst,"
*Forschungen und Fortschritte; Korrespondenzblatt der Deutschen
Wissenschaft und Technik,* XXXV (1961), 330-34, 375-79.

434 ———. "Das Alexander-Archiv und die Hellenistisch-Römische
Wissenschaft," *Historia,* X (1961), 30-67.

435 ———. "Eine Jüdische Gründungsgeschichte Alexandrias. Mit
einem Anhang über Alexanders Besuch in Jerusalem," *Akademie
der Wissenschaften, Heidelberg. Philosophisch-Historische
Klasse. Sitzungsberichte,* 1914, pp. 1-32.

436 ———. "Die Lokalhistorie von Sikyon bei Menaichmos Pausaneas
und den Chronographien," *Rheinisches Museum für Philologie,*
LXVIII (1913), 529-37. A genealogy of Pausanias.

437 ———. "Das Nachleben der Überlieferung von Alexander und
den Brahmanen," *Hermes; Zeitschrift für Klassische Philologie,*
LXXVI (1941), 143-69. A family tree for Alexander.

438 Picard, Charles. "Les Marins de Néarque et le Relais de l'Expédition d'Alexandre dans le Golfe Persique," *Revue Archéologique,*
I (1961), 60-65. A map of the Persian Gulf, many photographs,
and in addition to many notes, additional sources are listed in
the text.

439 ———. "Le Trône Vide d'Alexandre dans la Céremoine de
Cyinda et le Culte du Trône Vide à Traverse le Monde Gréco-
Romain," *Cahiers Archeologiques; Fin de l'Antiquité et Moyen Âge,*
VII (1954), 1-17. Quotations in Greek from ancient sources.

440 Pichon, René. "L'Époque Probable de Quinte-Curce," *Revue de Philologie, de Litterature et d'Histoire Anciennes*, XXXII (1908), 210-14.

441 Pietschmann, Richard. "Zu den Uberbleibseln des Koptischen Alexanderbuches," *Beiträge zur Bücherkunde August Wilmanns* (Leipzig, 1903), pp. 301-12.

442 Pincott, Frederic. "The Route by Which Alexander Entered India," *Royal Asiatic Society of Great Britain and Ireland, London. Journal*, Oct., 1894, pp. 677-89. One note with additional sources noted in the text; also, full-page map.

443 Pizzagalli, Angelo Maria. "Alessandro Magno e l'Ennismo," *Athene e Roma*, XXXVI (1934), col. 176-88.

444 ———. "Di un Giudizio del Manzoni Sopra un Anedotto della Vita di Alessandro," *Athene e Roma*, XIII (1911), col. 338-45. No notes but mentions ancient sources in the text; also long quotations from ancient sources.

445 Plassart, A. "Inscriptions de Delphes," *Bulletin de Correspondance Hellénique*, XXXVIII (1914), 101-88. The text of the inscriptions and translation; also photographs of the stones.

446 Plaumann, Gerhard. "Bemerkungen zu den Ägyptischen Eponymend aus Ptolemäischer Zeit," *Klio; Beiträge zur Alten Geschichte*, XIII (1919), 485-90. The text of an inscription and a plate.

447 ———. "Probleme des Alexandrinischen Alexanderkultes," *Archiv für Papryusforschung und Verwentegebiete*, VI (1920), 77-99. Comparisons of various texts.

448 Pohlenz, Max. "Kallimachos' Aitia," *Hermes; Zeitschrift für Klassische Philologie*, LXVIII (1933), 313-27. Quotations from classical sources.

449 Polotsvoff, N. "Iskander-Zulkarnain," *Forum*, LXXV (1926), 691-99. Line drawings; no notes.

450 Pomtow, H. "Delphica III: Die Krateroshalle (Alexanderjagd)," *Berliner Philologische Wochenschrift*, XXXII (1912), col. 1010-16. Various diagrams.

451 ———. "Delphische Neufunde," *Klio*; *Beiträge zur Alten Geschichte*, XIV (1914), 265-320. Quotations from ancient sources, texts of inscriptions, diagrams, chronological table of archons for 277/6-262/1, and a chronological table of events for 302-238 B.C.

452 ———. "Delphische Neufunde III," *Klio*; *Beiträge zur Alten Geschichte*, XVI (1927), 303-38. Diagrams and texts of inscriptions as well as illustrations.

453 Pottier, E. "Sur le Bronze du Musée de Naples Dit 'Alexandre à Cheval,' " *Mélanges Nicole*, 1905, pp. 427-43. Illustrations of the statue.

454 Powell, J. E. "The Sources of Plutarch's Alexander," *Journal of Hellenic Studies*, LIX (1939), 229-40. A section with textual notes on Plutarch and Arrian (in Greek). An abstract appears in the *American Journal of Archaeology*, XLIV (1940), 528.

455 Préaux, Claire. "Reflexions sur l'Entité Héllenistique," *Chronique d'Egypte*, XL (1965), 129-39.

456 Prentice, William Kelly. "Callisthenes, the Original Historian of Alexander," *American Philological Association. Transactions*, LIV (1923), 74-86. An undocumented article.

457 Prokesch- Osten, Baron de. "List des Alexandres de Ma Collection Qui ne se Trouvent pas dans le Catalogue de Mr. L. Müller," *Numismatische Zeitschrift*, 1869, 31-63. A catalog of coins with word descriptions of each and place of issue.

458 ———. "Suite des Monnaies Inédites d'Or et d'Argent d'Alexandre le Grand," *Numismatische Zeitschrift*, 1871, pp. 51-72. A catalog of coins.

459 ———. "Zwei Alexandermünzen," *Wiener Numismatische Monatschefte*, IV (1867), 6-8. No notes.

460 Pryce, F. N. "A Portrait of Alexander the Great," *British Museum Quarterly*, IX, no. 4 (1934-35), 134-35. Photographs; no notes but sources listed in the text.

461 Pugliese Carratelli, Giovanni. "Alessandro e la Costituzione
     Rodia," *La Parola del Passato*; *Rivista di Studi Classici*, IV
     (1949), 154-71.

462 Quatremère de Quincy, [Antoine Chrysostome]. "Memoire sur le
     Char Funéraire qui Transporta de Babylone en Égypte le Corps
     d'Alexandre, ou Projet de Restitution de ce Monument, d'après la
     Description de Diodore de Sicile," *Academie des Inscriptions
     et Belles-Lettres, Paris. Memoires*, IV (1818), pt. 2, 315-94. Two
     diagrams of the carriage, marginal notes and Greek and Latin
     quotations with French translations.

463 Radet, Georges. "Alexandre en Syrie. Les Offres de Paix que Lui
     Fit Darius," *Mélanges Syriens Offerts à Monsieur René Dus-,
     saud, Secrétaire Perpétuel de l'Académie des Inscriptions et
     Belles-Lettres, par Ses Amis et Ses Élèves*, I (1939), 235-47.

464 ————. "Alexandre et Poros; le Passage de l'Hydaspe," *Revue
     des Études Anciennes*, XXXVII (1935), 349-56, map. A compari-
     son of Stein's "The Site of Alexander's Passage of the Hydaspes
     and the Battle with Poros," and Breloer's *Alexanders Kampf
     gegen Porus*.

465 ————. "Aornos," *Journal des Savants*, 1929, pp. 69-73. Discussion
     concerning Stein's article "Alexander's Campaign in the Indian
     North-West Frontier" and of other English-language accounts.

466 ————. "La Consultation de l'Oracle d'Ammon par Alexandre,"
     *Brussels. Université Libre. Institut de Philologie et d'Histoire
     Orientales et Slaves. Annuaire*, II (1933-34), 779-92. Quotations
     in Greek from ancient sources.

467 ————. "La Deification d'Alexandre," *Revue des Universités du
     Midi*, I (1895), 129-69.

468 ————. "La Dernière Campagne d'Alexandre contre Darius,"
     Mélanges Gustave Glotz (Paris: Presses Universitaires de France),
     II (1932), 765-78. A bibliography and a map.

469 ————. "Les Idées et les Croyances d'Alexandre le Grand,"
     Journal des Savants, 1935, pp. 145-52.

470 ———. "Notes sur l'Histoire d'Alexandre," *Revue des Études Anciennes*, XXVII (1925), 11-14, 81-93, 183-208; XXVIII (1926), 113-20, 213-40; XXIX (1927), 5-34. A well-documented series of articles with a drawing and a map in the last segment.

471 ———. "Notes sur l'Histoire d'Alexandre IX," *Revue des Études Anciennes*, XLIII (1941), 33-40. A map.

472 ———. "Recherches sur la Geographie de l'Asia Mineure," *Revue des Études Anciennes*, V (1903), 1-14; VI (1904), 277-319; VIII (1906), 1-22; XII (1910), 365-72; XIX (1917), 98-100. A series of articles containing photographs, drawings, a map, and the 1904 section includes a catalog of "gemmes" with word descriptions of each type.

473 ———. "Sur les Traces d'Alexandre entre le Choès et l'Indus," *Journal des Savants*, 1930, pp. 207-27. A discussion of Stein's *On Alexander's Track to the Indus*. Contains a map.

474 ———. "La Valeur Historique de Quinte-Curce," *Academie des Inscriptions et Belles-Lettres, Paris. Comptes-Rendus des Seances,* 1924, pp. 356-65.

475 Ranovich, A. "Aleksandr Makedonskii i Grecheskiye Goroda Maloy Azii," (Alexander of Macedon and the Greek Cities of Asia Minor), *Akademiia Nauk, S.S.S.R. Institut Istorii. Vestnik Drevnei Istorii,* IV (1947), 57-63. Written in Russian.

476 Reinach, Adolphe. "Trophées Macédoniens," *Revue des Études Grecques*, XXVI (1913), 347-98. Illustrations and quotations in Greek from ancient sources.

477 Reinach, Salomon. "Deux Nouvelles Images d'Alexandre," *Revue Archéologique*, II (1906), 1-6. Six photographs of the two statues in question.

478 ———. "Une Statuette de Bronze Représentant Alexandre le Grand (Collection de M. Edmond de Rothschilde)," *Revue Archéologique*, 4th. ser., V (1905), 32-43.

479 Reinach, Théodore. "Un Fragment d'un Nouvel Historien d'Alexandre le Grand," *Revue des Études Grecques*, V (1892), 306-26.

Quotations in Greek from ancient sources and an appendix
containing various fragments with authors noted where known.

480 ———. "Les Sarcophages de Sidon au Musée de Constanople,"
Gazette des Beaux Arts, 3d. ser., VII (1892), 89-106; VIII
(1892), 177-95. Illustrated.

481 Reinmuth, O. W. "A New Text of the Correspondence of Alex-
ander with Dindimus and Aristotle," *American Philological
Association. Transactions and Proceedings,* LXXII (1941), xli.
An abstract of his paper presented before the Association.

482 Reitzenstein, Ricardus. "Arriani tōn met' Alexandron Libri Septimi
Fragmenta e Codice Vaticano Rescripto," *Breslauer Philologische
Abhandlungen,* III (1888), 1-36. The text of the inscription in
question.

483 Renard, Marcel and Servais, Jean. "A Propos du Mariage d'Alexandre et de Roxane," *Antiquite Classique,* XXIV (1955), 29-50.

484 Reuss, Friedrich. "Alexander der Grosse bei den Mallern,"
Bonner Jahrbucher, CXVIII (1909), 12-16. No footnotes; ancient
sources are cited in the text.

485 ———. "Hellenistische Beiträge,"*Rheinisches Museum für
Philologie,* LXII (1907), 591-600. No footnotes but sources are
mentioned in the text; quotations from ancient Greek sources.

486 ———. "Hellenistische Beiträge (Fortsetzung von Band LXII S.
591): 3 Kleitarchos," *Rheinisches Museum für Philologie,*
LXIII (1908), 58-78. No footnotes, but sources are cited in the
text; also a comparison of texts of Curtius (Latin), Diodorus
(Greek), and Plutarch (Greek.).

487 ———. "Jahresbericht über die Griechischen Historiker mit
Ausschluss des Herdot, Thukydides und Xenophon, 1900-1904,"
*Jahresbericht über die Fortschritte der Klassischen Altertum-
swissenschaft,* CXXVII (1905), 1-213. An annotated bibliography
of books for the period mentioned.

488 ———. "Der Leichenwagen Alexanders des Grossen,"
Rheinisches Museum für Philologie, LXI (1906), 408-13. No

footnotes, but sources are listed in the text; also quotations from ancient sources.

489 ———. "Zur Ueberlieferung der Geschichte Alexanders d. Gr.," *Rheinisches Museum für Philologie*, LVII (1902), 559-98. Few notes with additional sources in the text; a brief comparison of texts of Justin and Curtius.

490 Richards, G. C. "Proskynesis," *Classical Review*, XLVIII (1934), 168-70. No footnotes; sources are cited in the text.

491 Ritter, Carl. "Über Alexander des Grossen Feldzug am Indischen Kaukasus," *Akademie der Wissenschaften, Berlin. Historiographisch-Philologische Klasse. Abhandlungen*, 1829, pp. 137-74.

492 Rizzo, Giulio Emanuele. "La 'Battaglia di Alessandro,' " *Bollettino d'Arte nell'Arte Italica e Romana*, 2d. ser., V (1925-26), 529-46. Illustrations and notes at the end.

493 Robinson, Charles Alexander, Jr. "Alexander, Aristotle and the Brotherhood of Man," *Saturday Review*, July 25, 1942, 3-4, 15. An undocumented popular presentation of general information.

494 ———. "Alexander the Great and Parmenio," *American Journal of Archaeology*, 2d. ser., XLIX (1945), 422-24.

495 ———. "Alexander the Great and the Barbarians," *Classical Studies Presented to Edward Capps On His 70th. Birthday* (Princeton, 1936),pp. 298-305. Supports Tarn's theory that Alexander was inspired with the idea of the unity of mankind.

496 ———. "Alexander the Great and the Oecumene," *Hesperia. Supplement*, VIII (1949), 299-304.

497 ———. "Alexander the Great in India," *Geographical Review*, XXIII (1) (1933), 147. A brief and undocumented comment on Stein's article, "The Site of Alexander's Passage of the Hydaspes and the Battle with Porus," *Geographical Journal*, LXXX (1932), 31-46.

498 ———. "Alexander's Brutality," *American Journal of Archaeology*, 2d. ser., LVI (1952), 169-70. No footnotes; sources are cited in the text.

499 ———. "Alexander's Deification," *American Journal of Philology*, LXIV (1943), 286-301.

500 ———. "Alexander's Deification," *American Philological Association. Transactions and Proceedings*, LXXII (1941), xlii. An abstract of his paper presented before the Association.

501 ———. "Alexander's Descent of the Indus," *American Philological Association. Transactions and Proceedings*, LX (1929), xviii-xix. An abstract of his paper presented before the Association.

502 ———. "Alexander's Last Plans," *American Philological Association. Transactions*, LXIX (1938), xlvii. An abstract of his paper presented before the Association.

503 ———. "Alexander's Plans," *American Journal of Philology*, LXI (1940), 402-12. A list of plans taken from the writings of Diodorus.

504 ———. "The Extraordinary Ideas of Alexander the Great," *American Historical Review*, LXII (1957), 326-44.

505 ———. "The Historian Chares," *American Journal of Archaeology*, 2d. ser., XXXIII (1929), 99. Report of a paper read at general meeting of the Archaeological Institute of America in New York in 1928.

506 ———. "Motivation for Alexander's Universalism," *Studies Presented to David M. Robinson* (St. Louis: Washington University Press), II (1953), 830-32.

507 ———. "The Seer Aristander," *American Journal of Philology*, L (1929), 195-97. No footnotes; for a more lengthy and well-documented discussion the author refers to his doctoral dissertation.

508 ———. "The Seer Aristander," *American Philological Association. Transactions and Proceedings*, LIX (1928), xxv. An abstract of his paper presented before the Association.

509 ———. "Two Notes on the History of Alexander the Great," *American Journal of Philology*, LIII (1932), 353-59.

510 ———. "When Did Alexander Reach the Hindu Kush?," *American Journal of Philology*, LI (1930), 22-31. A chronology

of the life of Alexander (356- 323 B.C.), a more detailed accounting for 331 B.C., and a table illustrating the conclusions reached for February 330 to early summer of 327.

511 Robinson, David M. "The Alexander Hoard of Megalopolis," *Museum Notes*, IV (1950), 13-28. Six plates, many footnotes, and a list of issues by place and date with word descriptions.

512 ———. "A New Peloponnesian Hoard of Alexander and Ptolemaic Silver Coins," *American Journal of Archaeology*, 2d. ser., LIV (1950), 259-60. A description of the hoard with a discussion of the conclusions that can be drawn from its contents.

513 ———. "Unpublished Sculpture in the Robinson Collection," *American Journal of Archaeology*, LIX (1955), 19-29. Two illustrations.

514 ———. Rooy, C. A. van. "Die Problem van die Oorsprong van die Groot Alexandrynse Biblioteek," *Acta Classica*, I (1958), 147-61. Includes an English résumé.

515 Rostagni, Augusto. "Isocrate e Filippo," *Entaphia in Memoria di Emilio Pozzi la Scuola Torinese di Storia Antica* (Roma: Fratelli Bocca Editori, 1913), pp. 131-56.

516 Rostovtzeff, Michael Ivanovich. "The Foundations of Social and Economic Life in Egypt in Hellenistic Times," *Journal of Egyptian Archaeology*, VI (1920), 161-78. Text of a lecture presented before the Oxford Philological Society.

517 ———. "L'Hellénism en Mésopotame," *Scientia*, LIII (1933), 110-24.

518 ———. "The Hellenistic World and Its Economic Development," *American Historical Review*, XLI (1935-36), 231-52. Text of his Presidential Address delivered before the American Historical Association on December 28, 1935; a summary of a corresponding chapter in his book *Social and Economic History of Greece and the Hellenistic Monarchies after Alexander*. No footnotes. Available in German as "Die Hellenistische Welt und Ihre Wirtschaftliche Entwicklung," *Die Welt als Geschichte; Zeitschrift für Universalgeschichte*, IV (1938), 48-78.

519 ———. "The Near East in the Hellenistic and Roman Times," *Dumbarton Oaks Inaugural Lectures*, Nov. 2-3, 1940, pp. 27-40. One note.

520 ———. "L'Orient et la Civilisation Grecque; Doura-Europos sur l'Euphrate," *Renaissance*, I (1943), 43-59. Translated by H. Grégoire.

521 ———. "Seleucid Babylonia: Bullae and Seals of Clay with Greek Inscriptions," *Yale Classical Studies*, III (1930), 1-114. Contains many plates with verbal descriptions of the coins and seals; also a "Catalog of Impressions of Official Seals." Appended is a portion of a letter of Marino San Nicolo and brief essays by R. P. Dougherty and Robert H. McDowell.

522 Roussel, Pierre. "Alexandre Le Grand," *Journal des Savants*, Feb., 1932, pp. 49-60. An essay concerning Wilcken's *Alexander der Grosse* and Radet's *Alexandre le Grand*; a comparison.

523 ———. "Un Règlement Militaire de l'Époque Macédonienne," *Revue Archéologique*, 6th. ser., III-IV (1934), 39-47. A plate of the inscription and its text in Greek.

524 Rouvier, Jules. "L'Ère d'Alexandre le Grand en Phénicie aux IVᵉ et IIIᵉ Siècles avant J.-C.," *Revue des Études Grecques*, XI (1899), 362-81. A table of dates for coins and Phoenician dates.

525 ———. "L'Ère d'Alexandre le Grand en Phènicie (Note Complémentaire)," *Revue Numismatique*, 1903, pp. 239-51. A table of coins found in Phoenicia and dating from the period of Alexander (date, Alexandrine era, Greek letters, Phoenician letters, and place).

526 ———. "Nouvelles Recherches sur l'Ère d'Alexandre le Grand en Phénicie," *Revue Numismatique*, 1909, pp. 321-54.

527 Rubensohn, O. "Das Grab Alexanders des Grossen in Memphis," *Société Royale d'Archéologie d'Alexandrie. Bulletin*, 1910, pp. 83-86. Sources in the text in addition to the footnotes.

528 Rühl, Franz. "Alexandros und Sein Arzt Philippos," *Neue Jahrbücher für Philologie und Paedagogik*, CXXIII (1881), 361-64.

529 Ruggini, Lellia. "L'Epitoma Rerum Gestarum Alexandri Magni e il Liber de Morte Testamentoque Eius. (A Proposito della Recente Edizions di P. H. Thomas)," *Athenaeum*, XXXIX (1961), 285-357.

530 Sabbadini, Remigio. "La Lettera di Alessandro Magno ad Aristotele de Mirabilibus Indiae," *Rivista di Filologia e d'Istruzione Classica*, XV (1887), 534-36.

*531 Salač, A. "Alexander of Macedon and Al Iskandar Dhu-l-carnein," *Eunomia* (Praha), IV (1960), 41-43. Located at the University of Oxford, Bodleian Library.

532 Sălăc, Padává. "Sarapis a Efemeridy Alexandra Velikého, *Listy Filologické*, L (1923), 78-84.

533 Sallet, A. v. "Alexander der Grosse als Gründer der Baktrisch Indischen Reiche," *Zeitschrift für Numismatik*, VIII (1881), 279-80. Drawings of coins.

534 Samuel, Alan E. "Alexander's 'Royal Journals,' " *Historia*, XIV (1965), 1-12. The texts of the remaining fragments (in Greek) as reported by ancient authors.

535 Santerre, H. Gallet de. "Alexandre le Grand et Kymé d'Eolide," *Bulletin de Correspondance Hellénique*, 1947-8, pp. 302-06.

536 Scala, Rudolf von. "Das Griechischentum Seit Alexander dem Grossen," *Helmolts Weltgeschichte*, V (1904), 1-116. Printed in the old German type. A few notes, plates in color, and various family trees.

537 Schachermeyr, Fritz. "Alexander und die Ganges-Länder," *Innsbrucker Beiträge zur Kulturgeschichte*, III (1955), 123-35.

538 ———. "Das Ende des Makedonischen Königshauses," *Klio*; *Beiträge zur Alten Geschichte*, XVI (1920), 332-37. Quotations in Greek from ancient sources.

539 ———. "Zu Geschichte und Staatsrecht der Frühen Diadochenzeit," *Klio*; *Beiträge zur Alten Geschichte*, XIX (1925), 435-61. Quotations from ancient sources and a table of miliary commanders-in-chief.

540 ————. "Die Letzten Pläne Alexanders des Grossen," *Öster-reichischen Archäologischen Instituts. Jahreshefte*, XLI (1954), 118-40.

541 Schaefer, Arnold. "Analecta Philologica Historica. I.De Rerum Alexandri Magni Scriptorum Inprimis Arriani et Plutarchi Fontibus Disseruit Alfredus Schoene . . . ," *Neue Jahrbücher für Philologie und Paedagogik*, CI (1870), 433-46. A comparison of the texts of Arrian, Strabo, and Plutarch (in Greek).

542 Schehl, Franz. "Zum Korinthischen Bund vom Jahre 338/37 v. Chr.," *Oesterreichisches Archäologisches Institut, Wien. Jahreshefte*, XXVII (1931), 115-45. The text of inscriptions in Greek and numerous Greek quotations.

543 Schier, T. "Zur Lage des Schlachtfeldes von Issus und des Pinarus," *Wiener Studien*, XXXI (1909), 153-68. Many quotations from Arrian.

544 Schiwek, Heinrich. "Der Persische Golf als Schiffahrtsund Seehandelsroute in Achämenidischer Zeit und in der zeit Alexanders des Grossen," *Bonner Jahrbücher des Rhein*, CLXII (1962), 4-97. A bibliography in addition to its many notes.

545 Schjøtt, P. O. "König Alexander und die Makedonier," *Norske Videnskaps-Akademi, Oslo. Historisk-Filosofisk Klasse. Skrifter*, 1907, no. 6, pp. 1-27. A two-page fold-out plate.

546 Schnabel, Paul. "Die Begründung des Hellenistischen Königskults durch Alexander," *Klio; Beiträge zur Alten Geschichte*, XIX (1923/25), 113-27.

547 ————. "Zur Frage Selbstvergötterung Alexanders," *Klio; Beiträge zur Alten Geschichte*, XXIV (1926), 398-414. A comparison of the texts of Arrian and Plutarch.

548 Schneider, Rudolf. "Griechische Poliorketiker. III," *Akademie der Wissenschaften, Göttingen. Philologisch-Historische Klasse. Abhandlungen*, XII (1912), 1-87. Illustrations, texts of Greek inscriptions with German translations, and a Greek-word index.

549 Scholz, Gustav. "Die Militärischen und Politischen Folgen der Schlacht am Granikus," *Klio; Beiträge zur Alten Geschichte,* XV (1918), 199-214. Quotations in Greek from ancient sources.

550 Schöne, Richard. "Das Pompejanische Alexandermosiak," *Neue Jahrbücher für das Klassische Altertum, Geschichte und Deutsche Litteratur und für Pädagogik,* XXIX (1912), 181-204. Illustrated.

551 Schreider, Helen and Schreider, Frank. "In the Footsteps of Alexander the Great," *National Geographic Magazine,* CXXXIII (Jan., 1968), 1-65. Colored photographs, paintings, maps, but no notes. Narrative of the authors' trip retracing the steps of Alexander.

552 Schreiber, Theodor. "Studien über das Bildniss Alexander des Grossen," *Akademie der Wissenschaften, Leipzig. Philologisch-Historische Klasse. Abhandlungen,* XXI (1903), no. 3, 1-312. A table of contents, plates, quotations in Greek from ancient sources, name and place indexes, and an index of museums where the statues are housed.

553 Schubart, W. "Das Ptolemäerreich," *Der Alte Orient,* XXXV (1937), Heft 4, 1-39. A table of contents, short bibliography, and notes.

554 Schubert, R. "Die Porus-Schlacht," *Rheinisches Museum für Philologie,* LVI (1901), 543-62. No footnotes; classical sources are noted in the text.

555 Schuffert, ———. "Alexanders des Grossen. Indischer Feldzug," *Koenigliches Domgymnasium und Koenigl. Realgymnasium zu Colberg,* 1886, pp. 3-15. No notes; sources are mentioned in the text.

556 Schur, W. "Das Alexanderreich Nach Alexanders Tode," *Rheinisches Museum für Philologie,* LXXXIII (1934), 129-56.

557 Schwahn, Walther. "Zu IG. II 160 (Philipps Landfrieden)," *Rheinisches Museum für Philologie,* n.f., LXXVIII (1929), 188-98. The text of the inscription in Greek.

558 ————. "Die Nachfolge Alexanders des Grossen," *Klio*; *Beiträge zur Alten Geschichte*, XXIII (1930), 211-38; XXIV (1931), 306-32.

559 Schwartz, Eduard. "Kallisthenes Hellenika," *Hermes*; *Zeitschrift für Klassische Philologie*, XXXV (1900), 106-30. Extensive quotations from ancient sources.

560 Schwarz, Wilhelm. "Zur Politik Alexanders des Grossen," *Alexander the Great Pamphlets*, Duke University, no. 40, 12pp.

561 Segre, Mario. "Epigraphica VI. Epigramma Sepolcrale," *Societe Royale d'Archeologie d'Alexandrie. Bulletin*, XXXIV (1941), 27-39. Quotations in Greek from ancient sources and three illustrations.

562 Seltman, E. J. "Rare Gold Staters with Types of Alexander III," *Numismatische Zeitschrift*, 1913, pp. 203-210. Diagrams and word descriptions of the coins.

563 Severeanu, G. "Etude sur les Tétradrachmes Type Alexander le Grand, Frappés dans les Villes Pontiques de la Moesie Inferieure," *Societătii Numismatice Romăne. Buletinul*, XIX (1924). One note, but additional sources are cited in the text; also quotations from ancient sources.

564 ————. "Tetradrachme d'Alexandre le Grand Frappée par Dioscuridas," *Societatea Numismatica Romănă, Bucharest. Buletinul*, XXV-XXVI (1930-31), 14-16. Two views of the coin in question.

565 Sickenberger, Otto. "Was Wollte Alexander in Indien?," *Geistige Arbeit*; *Zeitung aus der Wissenschaften Welt*, XV (1942), 1-2. Sources are mentioned in the text.

566 Sinko, Tadeusz. "Wyprawa Aleksandra Wielkiego do Stratosfery: Batysfery," *Meander*; *Miesięcznik Poświęcony Kulturze Swiata Starozytnego*, III (3) (1948), 119-26. No notes; sources are mentioned in the text.

567 Six, J. "Apelleisches," *Deutsches Archaologisches Institut. Jahrbuch*, XXV (1910), 147-59. One small illustration of a coin.

568 ———. "Apelles," *Deutsches Archäologisches Institut. Jahrbuch,* XX (1905), 169-79. An illustration and quotations in Latin and Greek from ancient sources.

569 Sjöquist, Erik. "Alexander Herakles," *Boston. Museum of Fine Arts. Bulletin,* LI (1953), 30-33. Illustrated.

570 Smith, Vincent A. "The Position of the Autonomus Tribes of the Punjab Conquered by Alexander the Great," *Royal Asiatic Society of Great Britain and Ireland. Journal,* 1903, pp. 685-702.

571 Sneyders de Vogel, K. "L'Éducation d'Alexandre le Grand," *Neophilologus; a Modern Language Quarterly,* XXVIII (1942-43), 161-71. A photograph of the author.

572 Sokolowski, Ks. F. "Alexander Wielki Synem Bakchusa?," *Przeglad Historyczny,* XI (1934), 121-28, 300. A résumé of the article in French.

573 Sonklar, Carl von. "Die Schlacht bei Issus (333 vor Chr.)," *Organ der Militär-Wissenschaftlichen Vereine,* XII (1876), 185-201.

574 ———. "Die Schlacht von Arbela 331 vor Chr. G.," *Organ der Militär-Wissenschaftlichen Vereine,* XVI (1878), 161-77. Two illustrations and a list of soldiers with their leaders.

575 Speicker, Direktor. "Der Hof und die Hofordnung Alexanders d. Gr.," *Jahresbericht der Stadtischen Höheren Mädchenschule in Stolp i. P. Ostern,* II (1904), programm nr. 223, 1-22. Margin notes in addition to footnotes.

576 Stahl, A. F. von. "Notes on the March of Alexander the Great from Ecbatana to Hyrcania," *Royal Geographical Society of London. Geographical Journal,* LXIV (1924), 312-29.

577 Stark, Freya. "Alexander's March from Miletus to Phrygia," *Journal of Hellenic Studies,* LXXVIII (1958), 102-20. Four maps.

578 ———. "Alexander's Minor Campaigns in Turkey," *Geographical Journal,* CXXII (1956), 294-305. Text of a speech delivered on January 9, 1956, before the Royal Geographical Society. A map of the area and many photos but no footnotes.

579 Stark, K. B. "Zwei Alexanderköpfe der Sammlung Erbach und des Britischen Museums zu London," *Festschrift dem Kaiserlich Deutschen Archäologischen Institut zu Rom zur Fünfzigjährigen Stiftungsfeier*, 1879, pp. 1-21. Three photographs and sources in the text which supplement the footnotes.

580 Steele, R. B. "Curtius and Arrian," *American Journal of Philology*, XL (1919), 37-63, 153-74. Few notes but the first note has an extensive listings of sources, especially classical ones; also a discussion of the narrative common to Curtius and Arrian with a listing of specific passages.

581 ———. "Quintus Curtius Rufus," *American Journal of Philology*, XXXVI (1915), 402-23. No footnotes; ancient sources are mentioned in the text.

582 ———. "Quintus Curtius Rufus," *American Philological Association. Transactions and Proceedings*, XLIII (1912), LI-LIV. An abstract of a paper presented before the association; no footnotes, but sources are mentioned in the text.

583 ———. "Some Features of the Later Histories of Alexander," *Classical Philology*, XIII (July, 1918), 301-09. No footnotes; classical sources are cited extensively in the text, but no modern authors are mentioned.

584 Stein, Sir Aurel. "Alexander's Campaign on the Indian North-West Frontier," *Geographical Journal*, LXX (1927), 417-40, 515-40. A fold-out map, photographs of the area, a smaller map, and translations of passages of Arrian into English.

585 ———. "Notes on Alexander's Crossing of the Tigris and the Battle of Arbela," *Geographical Journal*, C (1942), 155-64. Maps and photograhps of the area.

586 ———. "On Alexander's Route into Gedrosia: an Archaeological Tour in Las Bela," *Geographical Journal*, CII (Nov.-Dec., 1943), 193-227. A map and many photos.

587 ———. "The Site of Alexander's Passage of the Hydaspes and the Battle with Poros," *Geographical Journal*, LXXX (July, 1932), 31-46. Photographs, a few footnotes, and additional sources cited in the text.

588 Steindorff, G.; Ricke, Herbert; Aubin, Hermann. "Der Orakel-tempel in der Ammonoase," *Zeitschrift für Aegyptische Sprache und Altertumskunde*, LXIX (1932), 1-24. Illustrations, quotations in Greek from ancient sources, heiroglyphic texts, diagrams, and many notes.

589 Stier, Hans Erich. "Zum Gottkönigtum Alexanders des Grossen," *Welt als Geschichte*; *Zeitschrift für Universalgeschichte*, V (1939), 391-95.

590 Stocks, H. "Ein Alexanderbrief in den Acta Cyriaci et Julittae," *Zeitschrift für Kirchengeschichte*, XXXI (1910), 1-47. Comparisons of various ancient sources.

591 Stocks, J. L. "The Composition of Aristotle's Politics," *Classical Quarterly*, XXI (1927), 177-87.

592 Strasburger, Hermann. "Alexanders Zug durch Gedrosische Wüste," *Hermes*; *Zeitschrift für Klassische Philologie*, LXXX (1952), 456-93. Subject guides to the text are given in the margins.

593 ———. "Zur Route Alexanders durch Gedrosien," *Hermes*; *Zeitschrift für Klassische Philologie*, LXXXII (1954), 251-54.

594 Stroux, Johannes. "Die Stoische Beurteilung Alexanders des Grossen," *Philologus*, LXXXVIII (1933), 222-40.

595 ———. "Die Zeit des Curtius," *Philologus*, LXXXIV (n.f., XXXVIII) (1928), 233-51. In addition to notes, sources are mentioned in the text; quotations in Greek and Latin from ancient sources.

596 Studniczka, Franz. "Über die Grundlagen der Geschichtlichen Erklärung der Sidonischen Sarkophage (Mit einer Beilage)," *Deutsches Archäologisches Institut. Jahrbuch*, IX (1894), 204-44. Photographs, drawings, and a diagram of the tomb.

597 "The Successors of Alexander and Greek Civilization in the East," *Quarterly Review*, CXLIX (1880), 66-83. A good but undocumented survey of Hellenistic life based upon J. G. Droysen's *Geschichte des Hellenismus* (2d. ed. Halle, 1877-78), G. Lumbroso's *L'Economie Politiqué de l'Egypte sous les Lagides* (Turin, 1870), Von Wolfgang Helbig's *Untersuchungen über die*

Campanische Wandmalerei (Leipzig, 1873), and Major-General A. Cunningham's "The Numismatic Chronicle."

598 Suhr, Elmer G. "Sculptured Portraits of Greek Statesmen; with a Special Study of Alexander the Great," *Johns Hopkins University. Studies in Archaeology*, XIII (1931), 1-139. A collection of sculptured portraits from the earliest stages of Greek history to Roman times. Includes a list of illustrations, a bibliography, and many plates.

599 Sumner, G. V. "Curtius Rufus and the 'Historiae Alexandri,' " *A.U.M.L.A.*, XV (1961), 30-39. A brief biography of Curtius.

600 Supka, G. "Beiträge zur Darstellung Luftfahrt Alexanders des Grossen," *Zeitschrift für Christliche Kunst*," XXVI (1911), 307-14. Four illustrations.

601 Susemihl, Francisci. "Analectorum Alexandrinorum Chronologicorum," *Index Scholarum in Universitate Litteraria Gryphiswaldensi per Semestre Hibernum Anni MDCCCLXXXVIII-LXXXIX* (Greifswald: Typis Iulii Abel, 1888). Notes and a chronological table.

602 Sykes, Percy. "Alexander the Great as an Explorer," *Nineteenth Century and After*, CII (Oct., 1927), 565-73.

603 Taeger, Fritz. "Alexander der Grosse und die Anfänge des Hellenistischen Heerscherkultes," *Historische Zeitschrift*, CLXXII (1951), 225-44.

604 ————. "Alexanders Gottkönigsgedanke und die Bewusstseinslage der Griechen und Makedonien," *The Sacral Kingship. Contributions to the Central Theme of the VIIIth. International Congress for the History of Religions* (Leiden: E. J. Brill, 1959), pp. 394-406.

605 ————. "Isokrates und die Anfänge des Hellenistischen Herrscherkultes," *Hermes; Zeitschrift für Klassische Philologie*, LXXII (1937), 355-60. Quotations in Greek from ancient sources.

606 ————. "West und Ost im Hellenismus," *Hessische Blätter für Volkskunde*, XLI (1950), 14-33.

607 Tamás, Pekáry. "A 'Collatio Alexandri Magni et Dindimi,' " *Antik Tanulmányok. Studia Antiqua*, III (1956), 105-16.

608 Tarn, William Woodthrope. "Alexander and the Ganges," *Journal of Hellenic Studies*, XLIII (1943), 93-101. The conclusion of a study dealing with Diodorus; author's attempt to discredit the legend preserved by Diodorus.

609 ———. "Alexander, Cynics and Stoics," *American Journal of Philology*, LX (1939), 41-70. Presents the idea that Alexander's universalism predated the Stoic conception of the same idea.

610 ———. "Alexander the Great," *Classical Review*, XLVI (1932), 216-17. A comparison of Wilcken's *Alexander the Great* and Robinson's *The Ephemerides of Alexander's Expedition*.

611 ———. "Alexander the Great and the Unity of Mankind," *British Academy for the Promotion of Historical, Philosophical, and Philological Studies. Proceedings*, XIX (1933), 123-66. A Raleigh Lecture on History delivered on May 10, 1933. An extraordinary number of notes and a discussion of the probable date of the writer Euhemerus.

612 ———. "Alexander's Hypomnemata and the 'World Kingdom,' " *Journal of Hellenic Studies*, XLI (1921), 1-17. A discussion of items in Diodorus 18, 2-4 that are not in Hieronymus.

613 ———. "Alexander's Plans," *Journal of Hellenic Studies*, LIX (1939), 124-35.

614 ———. "The Hellenistic Ruler-Cult and the Daemon," *Journal of Hellenic Studies*, XLVIII (1928), 206-19.

615 ———. "The Massacre of the Branchidae," *Classical Review*, XXXVI (1922), 63-6. His views were later questioned by L. R. Farnell; see *JHS* XLIX (1929), 79-81.

616 ———. "Notes on Hellenism in Bactria and India," *Journal of Hellenic Studies*, XVI (1902), 268-93. A photographic reproduction of bronze coins.

617 Taylor, Lily Ross. "Alexander and the Serpent of Alexandria," *Classical Philology*, XXV (1930), 375-78.

618 ———."The Cult of Alexander at Alexandria," *Classical Philology*, XXII (1927), 162-69.

619 ———. "The 'Proskynesis' and the Hellenistic Ruler Cult," *Journal of Hellenic Studies*, XLVII (1927), 53-62.

620 Teplow, M. W. "Recherches sur l'Emplacement du Champ de Bataille au Passage du Granique," *Académie des Inscriptions et Belles-Lettres. Memoires Présentés par Divers Savants*, 1st. ser., X (1893), pt. 1, 217-33. A map.

621 Thiersch, H. "Die Alexandrinische Königsnekropole," *Deutsches Archäologisches Institut. Jahrbuch*, XXV (1910), 55-97. Quotations from ancient sources.

622 ———. "Lysipps Alexander Mit der Lanze," *Deutsches Archäologisches Institut. Jahrbuch*, XXIII (1908), 162-69. Four illustrations and quotations from Plutarch.

623 Thomas, C. G. "Alexander the Great and the Unity of Mankind," *Classical Journal*, LXIII (1968), 258-60.

624 Thomes, Franco Carrata. "Il Problema degli Eteri nella Monarchia di Alessandro Magno," *Torino. Università. Facoltà di Lettere e Filosofia. Pubblicazioni*, VII (1955), Fasc. 4. Entire issue contains a series of articles by the author. A name index, an index of sources cited, and a listing of testimony of primary sources on various subjects.

625 Thompson, Margaret and Bellinger, Alfred R. "Greek Coins in the Yale Collection, IV: A Hoard of Alexander Drachms," *Yale Classical Studies*, XIV (1955), 3-45. Many plates of coins and a conspectus of Alexandrine issues for the following locations: Lampsacus, Abydus, Teos, Colophon, Magnesia, Miletus, and Sardes. Includes date of issue and a word description of each coin.

626 Tibiletti, Gianfranco. "Alessandro e la Liberazione delle Città d'Asia Minore," *Athenaeum*, n.s., XXXII (1954), 3-22.

627 Todd, Richard A. "W. W. Tarn and the Alexander Ideal," *Historian*, XXVII (1964), 48-55. A brief biographical note about Tarn and a discussion of his works.

628 Tondriau, Julien L. "Alexandre le Grand Assimilé à Differentes Divinités," *Revue de Philologie*, XXIII (1949), 41-52. A list of sources concerning each diety.

629 ———. "Bibliographie des Souverains Hellénistes et Romains," *Association Guillaume Budé. Bulletin*, 2d. ser., V (1948), 106-25. An unannotated listing which includes both books and periodical articles; divided by country and by person.

630 ———. "Comparisons and Identifications of Rulers with Deities in the Hellenistic Period," *Review of Religion*, XIII (1948), 24-47.

631 Toussoun, *Prince* Omar. "Note sur le Voyage d'Alexandre le Grand à l'Oasis de Jupiter Ammon (Siwa)," *Institut d'Egypte, Cario. Bulletin*, 6th. ser., XVI (1933/34), 77-83. The undocumented text of a lecture presented before the Institute on Feb. 5, 1934; with a double map.

632 Tcherikover, V. (Avigdor). "Die Hellenistischen Städtegründungen von Alexander dem Grossen bis auf die Römerzeit," *Philologus. Supplementband*, XIX (1927), 1-216. Contains many notes but no bibliography; subject and name indexes. Contains a comparison of place names in "Alterorientalischer," "Hellenistischer," and modern name; also lists of Hellenistic states according to Arrian.

633 Treves, P. "Hyperides and the Cult of Hephaestion," *Classical Review*, LIII (1939), 56-57.

634 Unger, G. F. "Der Attische Schaltkreis," *Philologus*, XXXIX (1880), 475-526. A chronological table, comparisons of the texts of Pluarch and Arrian, and quotations in Greek of ancient sources.

635 Usener, Hermann. "Divus Alexander," *Rheinisches Museum für Philologie*, LVII (1902), 171-73. Reprinted in *Kleine Schriften*, IV (1913), 396-98.

636 Vallois, R. "Alexandre et la Mystique Dionysiaque," *Revue des Études Anciennes*, XXXIV (1932), 81-2.

637 ———. "L'Oracle Libyen et Alexandre," *Revue des Études Grecques*, XLIV (1931), 121-52. Quotations from ancient sources.

638 Vaux, W. S. W. "Extract of a Letter from Charles T. Newton, Esq., Her Majesty's Vice Consul at Mytilene, to Mr. Burgon, of

the British Museum, Chiefly Relating to a Hoard of Coins of Alexander the Great, Discovered Near Patras in 1850," *Numismatic Chronicle and Journal of the Royal Numismatic Society*, XVI (1853/54), 29-37. Text of a letter read before the Numismatic Society on May 27, 1852. Coins are listed by class with word descriptions and illutsrations.

639 Veith, Georg. "Der Kavalleriekampf in der Schlacht am Hydaspes," *Klio; Beiträge zur Alten Geschichte*, VIII (1908), 131-53.

640 Vellay, Charles. "Alexandre en Troade," *Acropole; Revue du Monde Hellenique*, VI (1931), 119-28.

641 Vogel, A. "Die Quellen Plutarchs in der Biographie Alexanders des Grossen," *Kaiserliches Lyceum in Colmar. Programm Womit zu der Öffentlichen Prüfung am 10. und 11. August 1877* (Colmar: Buchdruckerei von Wittwe Camille Decker, 1877), pp. 1-18.

642 Vogt, Joseph. "Die Tochter des Grosskönigs und Pausanias, Alexander, Caracalla," *Satura. Früchte aus der Antiken Welt*, ed. by Otto Weinrich (Baden-Baden: Verlag für Kunst und Wissenschaft, 1952), 163-82.

643 Vulič, N. "Alexander's Zug gegen die Triballer," *Klio; Beiträge zur Alten Geschichte*, IX (1909), 490-91.

*644 ———."Alexandre-le-Grand sur le Danube," *Xenia, Hommage International à l'Université Nationale de Grèce* (Athens, 1912).

645 Wachsmuth, C. "Bemerkungen zu Griechischen Historikern," *Rheinisches Museum für Philologie*, LVI (1901), 215-26. Quotations from ancient sources.

646 ———. "Zur Metzer Alexander-Epitome," *Rheinisches Museum für Philologie*, LVI (1901), 150-54.

647 Waddington, W.-H. "Trouvailles de Saïda et de Marmari," *Revue Numismatique*, 1865, pp. 1-28.

648 Waele, F. J. M. de. "Het Westen in het Veroveringsplan van Alexander de Groote," *Vlaamische Academie voor Wetenschappen, Letteren en Schoone Kunsten van België. Klasse der Letteren.*

Mededeelingin, VI(2) (1944), 5-32. A bibliography; notes are collected at the end.

649 Walbank, F. W. "Surety in Alexander's Letter to the Chians," *Phoenix,* XVI (1962), 178-80.

650 Walser, Gerold. "Zur Neueren Forschung über Alexander den Grossen," *Schweizer Beiträge zur Allgemeinen Geschichte,* XIV (1956), 156-89. A separate bibliography in addition to many footnotes.

651 Walter, F. "Zum Itinerium Alexandri," *Philologus,* LXXXVII(4), (1932), 480. A brief undocumented note.

652 Wardman, A. E. "Plutarch and Alexander," *Classical Quarterly,* n.s., V (1955), 96-107. Many quotations from Plutarch in Greek.

653 Welles, C. Bradford. "Alexander's Historical Achievement," *Greece and Rome,* 2d. ser., XII (1965), 216-28. A fold-out map of Alexander's travels.

654 ———. "The Discovery of Sarapis and the Foundation of Alexandria," *Historia,* XI (1962), 271-98. A long list of sources in the first of many notes.

655 West, M. L. "An Epic Fragment in Servius," *Classical Review,* n.s., XIV (1964), 242. A very brief note with no documentation.

656 Wheeler, Benjamin Ide. "Alexander in Anger and in Love. Alexander the Great: Ninth Paper," *Century Magazine,* LVIII (1899), 396-409. Many drawings.

657 ———. "Alexander in Egypt. Alexander the Great: Seventh Paper," *Century Magazine,* LVIII (1899), 24-38. Drawings, a map of Alexandria, and some notes.

658 ———. "Alexander the Great. His Boyhood and the Assassination of Philip," *Century Magazine,* LVII (1898/99), 1-24. Many photographs and drawings, a map, but no notes.

659 ———. "Alexander the Great. His Victories in Thrace, Illyria, and Greece," *Century Magazine,* LVII (1898/99), 202-19. Many photographs and drawings, but few notes.

660 ———. "Alexander the Great. The Invasion of Asia and the
Battle of Granicus," *Century Magazine*, LVII (1898/99), 354-73.
Many drawings and photographs, a map, a plan of the battle of
the Granicus, and one note.

661 ———. "Alexander's Conquest of Asia Minor. Alexander the
Great: Fourth Paper," *Century Magazine*, LVII (1898/99),
554-71. Photographs, drawings, and a footnote.

662 ———. "Alexander's Death. Alexander the Great: Concluding
Paper," *Century Magazine*, LVIII (1899), 900-11. Drawings
and one note.

663 ———. "Alexander's Invasion of India. Alexander the Great:
Tenth Paper," *Century Magazine*, LVIII (1899), 525-39. Many
drawings and photographs.

664 ———. "Alexander's Mightiest Battle. Alexander the Great:
Eighth Paper," *Century Magazine*, LVIII (1899), 230-44. A plan
of battle for Gaugamela, a map, and some notes.

665 ———. "Alexander's Return from India: Eleventh Paper,"
Century Magazine, LVIII (1899), 764-78. Drawings, photographs,
and maps.

666 ———. "Alexander's Victory at Issus. Alexander the Great: Fifth
Paper," *Century Magazine*, LVII (1898/99), 678-91. Photographs,
drawings, a plan of the battle of Issus, and one footnote.

667 ———. "The Famous Siege of Tyre. Alexander the Great: Sixth
Paper," *Century Magazine*, LVII (1898/99), 818-31. Many
drawings, a map, and one note.

668 Wiedemann, Th. "Über das Zeitalter des Geschichtsschreibers
Curtius Rufus," *Philologus*, XXX (1870), 241-64, 441-43; XXXI
(1872), 342-48, 551-62, 756-68. Comparisons of texts of Curtius
with Tacitus, Seneca, Diodirus; Tacitus and Dio, and of
Plutarch and Seneca.

669 Wilamowitz-Moellendorff, Ulrich von. "Alexander der Grosse,"
Reden aus der Kriegszeit, XI (Heft 5) (1916), 1-40. Text of a
speech, set in the old German type; no footnotes or index.

670 ———. "Der Leichenwagen Alexanders des Grossen," *Deutsches Archäologisches Institut. Jahrbuch*, XX (1905), 103-08.

671 Wilcken, Ulrich. "Alexander der Grosse und der Korinthische Bund," *Akademie der Wissenschaften, Berlin. Philosophisch-Historische Klasse. Sitzungsberichte*, XVI (1922), 97-118. Quotations from ancient sources.

672 ———. "Alexander der Grosse und die Hellenistische Wirtschaft," *Schmollers Jahrbuch für Gesetzgebung Verwaltung und Volkswirtschaft im Deutschen Reich*, XLV (1921), 349-420. A series of seven articles printed in the old German type.

673 ———. "Alexander der Grosse und die Indischen Gymnosophisten," *Akademie der Wissenschaften, Berlin. Philologisch-Historische Klasse. Sitzungsberichte*, XVII (1923), 150-83. Comparisons of the texts of fragments.

674 ———. "Alexanders Zug in die Oase Siwa," *Akademie der Wissenschaften, Berlin. Philosophisch-Historische Klasse. Sitzungsberichte*, 1928, pp. 576-603.

675 ———. "Alexanders zug zum Ammon; Ein Epilog," *Akademie der Wissenschaften, Berlin. Philosophisch-Historische Klasse. Sitzungsberichte*, X (1930), 159-76. Quotations from ancient sources.

676 ———. "Beiträge zur Geschichte des Korinthischen Bundes," *Akademie der Wissenschaften, Munich. Philosophische-Historische Klasse. Sitzungsberichte*, X (1917), 1-40. Quotations from ancient sources in Greek.

677 ———. "Zur Entstehung des Hellenistischen Königskultes," *Akademie der Wissenschaften, Berlin. Philosophisch-Historische Klasse. Sitzungsberichte*, XVIII (1938), 298-321.

678 ———. "Hypomnematismoi," *Philologus*, LIII (1894), 80-126. Reprinting of fragments in Greek and a comparison of the texts of Arrian and Plutarch.

679 ———. "Kaiserliche Tempelverwaltung in Aegypten," *Hermes; Zeitschrift für Klassische Philologie*, XXIII (1888), 592-606. Extensive quotations in Greek from ancient sources.

680 ———. "Die Letzten Pläne Alexanders des Grossen," *Akademie der Wissenschaften, Berlin. Philosophisch-Historische Klasse. Sitzungsberichte*, XVII (1937), 192-207.

681 Wilhelm, Adolf. "Ein Neues Bruchstück der Parischen Marmorchronik," *Deutsches Archäologisches Institut. Athenische Abteilung. Mitteilungen*, XXII (1897), 183-217. A fold-out reproduction of the inscription with a transcription into modern Greek by Michael K. Krispi, also a discussion of its segments.

682 Willrich, Hugo. "Krateros und der Grabherr des Alexandersarkophags von Sidon," *Hermes; Zeitschrift für Klassische Philologie*, XXXIV (1899), 231-50.

683 Winter, Franz. "Die Sarkophage von Sidon," *Archaeologischer Anzeiger*, IX (1894), 1-23. Illustrations, diagrams, and plans.

684 Wirth, Gerhard. "Anmerkungen zur Arrianbiographie; Appian-Arrian-Lukian," *Historia*, XIII (1964), 209-45. Many long quotations from the texts of Appian, Arrian, and Lucian.

685 Wit, C. de. "Voyage à l'Oasis d'Ammon," *La Nouvelle Clio*, X-XII (1958-62), 272-73. A brief discussion (undocumented) of the author's visit of the area in November, 1958.

686 Wlad, Stanislaus. "Der Zug Alexanders des Grossen nach dem Fünfstromlande," *Jahresbericht des K. K. Zweiten Staatsgymnasiums in Czernowitz*, XV (1912), 1-32. Diagrams and maps.

687 Wüst, Fritz Rudolf. "Zu den Hypomnemata Alexanders des Grossen: Das Grabmal des Hephaistion," *Oesterreichisches Archäologisches Institut. Jahreshefte*, XLIV (1959), 147-57. Quotations from ancient sources.

688 ———. "Die Rede Alexanders des Grossen in Opis, Arrian VII 9-10," *Historia*, II (1953/54), 177-88. Many long quotations from Arrian in Greek.

689 ———. "Die Meuterei von Opis (Arrian VII, 8; II, 1-7)," *Historia*, II (1935/54), 418-31.

690 Ziegler, Konrat. "Plutarchstudien," *Rheinisches Museum für Philologie*, LXXXIV (1935), 369-90. Quotations from ancient sources, but only two notes.

691 Zimmermann, Rudolf. "Die Zeit des Geschichtsschreibers Curtius Rufus," *Rheinisches Museum für Philologie*, LXXIX (1930), 381-90. A bibliography in the text and quotations in Latin from ancient sources.